BLESSED HARBOURS

AN ANTHOLOGY OF
HUNGARIAN-CANADIAN AUTHORS

PROSE SERIES 65

ONTARIO ARTS COUNCIL
CONSEIL DES ARTS DE L'ONTARIO

Canadä

Guernica Editions Inc. acknowledges support of
The Canada Council for the Arts.
Guernica Editions Inc. acknowledges support from the Ontario Arts Council.
Guernica Editions Inc. acknowledges the financial support of the
Government of Canada through the Book Publishing Industry Development
Program (BPIDP).

BLESSED HARBOURS

AN ANTHOLOGY OF
HUNGARIAN-CANADIAN AUTHORS

EDITED BY JOHN MISKA

GUERNICA
TORONTO·BUFFALO·CHICAGO·LANCASTER (U.K.)
2002

John Miska, Guest editor
Guernica Editions Inc.
P.O. Box 117, Station P, Toronto (ON), Canada M5S 2S6
2250 Military Road, Tonawanda, N.Y. 14150-6000 U.S.A.

Distributors:
University of Toronto Press Distribution,
5201 Dufferin Street, Toronto (ON), Canada M3H 5T8
Independent Publishers Group,
814 N. Franklin Street, Chicago, Il. 60610 U.S.A.
Gazelle Book Services,
Falcon House, Queen Square, Lancaster LA1 1RN U.K.

First edition.
Typeset by Selina.
Printed in Canada.

Legal Deposit — Second Quarter
National Library of Canada
Library of Congress Catalog Card Number: 2002102766
National Library of Canada Cataloguing in Publication Data
Main entry under title:
Blessed harbours : an anthology of Hungarian-Canadian authors
(Prose series ; 65)
ISBN 1-55071-171-7
1. Canadian literature (English) — Hungarian-Canadian authors.
I. Miska, John P., 1932- II. Series.
PS8235.H8B58   2002   C810.8'0894511   C2002-900483-7
PR9194.5.H8B58   2002

CONTENTS

ACKNOWLEDGEMENTS

Joseph Csinger. The poems published in this volume were taken from his *Keyhole in the Sky*, Microform Biblios, Victoria, B.C., 1998.

Dobozy, Tamas. "Red Love" first appeared in *Chicago Review*, the publisher of the University of Chicago, 41, no 4, 1995.

Alex Domokos. "The Prisoner's Gift" first appeared in the *Canadian Fiction Magazine. Translation Issue 1*, edited by Charles Lillard and Geoffrey Hancock, 1976.

Ferenc Fáy. The English version of "Sunflower" first appeared in *CV II*, edited by Dorothy Livesay, December 1976.

George Faludy. The poems included here were taken from his *Selected Poems*, 1933-1980. Edited and translated by Robin Skelton. Toronto: McClelland & Stewart, 1985.

Maria Green. "Of Birds and Jews" first appeared in *Canadian Fiction Magazine. Translation Issue 1*, edited by Charles Lillard and Geoffrey Hancock, 1976.

Endre Farkas. "I Love You" first appeared in his *Here to Here*. Montreal: The Muses' Company, 1982.

George Jonas. The poems reproduced here come from his *East Wind Blows West*. Vancouver: Cacanadada,1993.

Judith Kalman. "The New World" first appeared in *Queen's Quarterly 104*, no. 3 (Fall, 1997).

László Kemenes Géfin. "The Importance of Becoming a Boy Scout" first appeared in *Canadian Fiction Magazine*. Translation Issue 1, edited by Charles Lillard and Geoffrey Hancock, 1976.

John Marlyn. "Good for You, Mrs. Feldesh" first appeared in *Dalhousie Review* 60 1980-1981.

Marina McDougall (Mezey). "The Echo Princess," based on a Hungarian legend, first appeared in *Canadian Children's Annual*, Potlatch Publications, 1979.

George Payerle. "London Scenes" was published in his *Unknown Soldier*, published by Macmillan of Canada, 1987.

Éva Sárvári. "During Office Hours" first appeared in English translation in *Canadian Fiction Magazine. Translation Issue* 1, edited by Charles Lillard and Geoffrey Hanckock, 1976.

Jim Tallosi. The poems reproduced here first appeared in his *The Trapper and the Fur-faced Spirits*. Winnipeg: Queenston House, 1981.

Eva Tihanyi. "Acrobatics" first appeared in her *A Sequence of the Blood*, Toronto: Aya Press, 1982; "Death Song" was taken from her *Prophecies Near the Speed of Light*, Saskatoon: Thistledown Press, 1984, and "My Grandmother's Gloves" comes from her *Restoring the Wickedness*, Saskatoon: Thistledown, 2000.

Robert Zend. "Oab's Lullaby" first appeared in his *Oab*, vol. 2, Toronto: Exile, 1985.

The Editor wishes to express thanks to the above publishers for their kind permission to reproduce the poems and short stories in this volume. The title of the anthology comes from the title of a poem, which is also the title of one of Iván Béky-Halász' collection of poems, *Áldott kikötők* (Blessed Harbours), published in 1979.

JOHN MISKA

Preface

This anthology, the second in this series (the first collection, entitled *The Sound of Time*, was published in 1974), includes selections from the works of Hungarian-Canadian writers. The purpose is to keep the reader abreast of current literary trends created by this nationality. Some of the poems and short stories included were originally written in English, but the majority were translated from the Hungarian.

The criteria for inclusion were based on a number of considerations. The authors had to be of Hungarian descent and representing the generations from the beginning of the last century; they had to be citizens or residents of Canada at the time the works were written, and the emphasis was placed upon the literary and aesthetic value of a piece considered for publication. The process of selection has been a careful undertaking as, according to our bibliographic records, there are more than a hundred authors of Hungarian origin in this country who have published books of poems, short stories, novels and plays.

The collection is arranged alphabetically by author. The volume also provides an overview of Hungarian-Canadian literature, as well as biographical notes and a select list of references in English pertaining to Hungarian-Canadian literature.

As far as literary styles and genre are concerned, represented are a variety of schools of poetry and fiction from the Hungarian Occidentalist school to the classicist movement, to surrealism, to neo-dadaism and mystical populism, most of which are still alive and flourishing, especially surrealism and neo-dadaism, owing to the increasing number of works by younger generation poets. The latter show signs of rejection of traditional literary values and have developed a rich variety of forms and texture, a poetic genre characterized by sensuous surrealistic imagery.

The prose writers, writing in Hungarian or English, also represent a variety of traditions, some of them employing the retrospective method by placing home-country experiences within Canadian frames. Those making English their creative language are familiar to the English-speaking reader.

Hungarian-Canadians may find it natural that poetry appears to be the stronger domain of their literature. It can be attributed to the rich poetic traditions dating back to the 16th century, when such poets as Bálint Balassi surfaced as the first accomplished lyricists in the Magyar language. In addition to poetry, Hungarian poets appear to be more courageous at taking risks in experimentation with form and exploration of theme than prose writers, responding to the reverberations of the soul that is undergoing the very subjective qualities of trauma, uprooting and relocation. In addition, writing lasting fiction requires intimate relationship with the land, a fact that takes time to develop.

A close look at the literary output in the Hungarian language indicates that Hungarian-Canadian novelists and short story writers, with the exception of the younger ones, favour drawing their themes from the distant past, reminiscences of home and childhood. If they venture to touch upon contemporary events, it is with emphasis upon life situations and minutiae of personal events at the expense of more consequential and personal experience.

This trend, however, is not confined to Hungarian-Canadian fiction writing alone; it is a noticeable phenomenon suppressing modern prose writing in general. For decades, the English and American critics have been drawing attention to the decline of the English-language novel. After the great flourishing of fiction in the relatively stable nineteenth century, the successive cataclysms of the first half of the twentieth century left most novelists stranded in confusion and spiritual doubt. Similarly, an air of stagnation pervades fictive prose in Hungary as well. The panoramic historical and social novels of Zsigmond Móricz, Péter Veres and Tibor Déry, to mention but a few, have given way to brooding short novels that are concerned with escape from the emotional tangles of present personal life in that country.

Similar trends can be detected in English and French-Canadian authors who, influenced by proponents of the individualist school, are growing increasingly estranged from the rich legacy of this nation's literature. The historical and regional novels fashionable in the 1920s, the marcant naturalism of the 1930s, the penetrating realistic novels of the 1940s and 1950s all in turn have vanished, giving way to focusing on disparate aspects of our time. In spite of an apparent setback in this genre, however, there is an increasing tendency in new literary explorations amongst Canadian writers, a fact being also evident in the prose section of this collection.

As far as thematic values of Hungarian-Canadian literature are concerned, it would be quite easy to map Canada and Hungary based on poetry and fiction written by Hungarian-Canadians. The authors are most sensitive to their environment; their fiction and poems are full of references to Canadian settings from Atlantic Canada to the rain forests of British Columbia.

It has been suggested by students of multiculturalism that most human experiences, and it is particularly true in the case of displaced people, originate from the presence of loneliness. Loneliness, one might say, the lacking of a satisfying social contact is ever present in Hungarian-Canadian literature. The short stories and poems represented here are an example of the intent of their authors and their proponents to express their desire for meaningful human relations, a condition so allusive in our lifestyles, a desire so well portrayed in these writings.

This anthology has been in the making for a decade. In the meantime, some of its writers have passed away, a few of them have returned to their native land, but most of them made Canada their homeland. The editor would like to express gratitude to a great number of people who so enthusiastically contributed their time and talent. His special thanks go to Genevieve Bartole, John Robert Colombo, Joaquim Kuhn, Dennis Lee, Christopher Levenson, George Payerle, Karl Sandor, Erika Simon, and the late Robin Skelton for doing the final translations of the poems originally written in Hungarian.

A vote of thanks to Peter Kaslik, Michael Nogrady, and Maxim Tabory, as well as to the authors of the vernacular writings for their assistance in the preparation of the literal translations. Our special thanks go to Guernica Editions for publishing *Blessed Harbours*.

Victoria, B.C., January 2000

GEORGE BISZTRAY

Their Language Is Their Destiny

Hungarian-Canadian literature is a relatively recent phenomenon, although Hungarian immigration to Canada began more than a hundred years ago. The first settlers were farmers on the Saskatchewan prairie who already held poetry in high esteem. The first collection of Hungarian poems was written in Canada by a general store manager of Békevár-Kipling called Gyula Izsák. It was published in 1919 under the appropriate title *Prairie Flowers* (Mezei virágok).

The poetry and prose written before World War II have not been assessed yet. Many of these works still exist in manuscript form only, or are awaiting re-discovery on the pages of old Hungarian-Canadian newspapers. Based on the limited volume of already published materials, however, we can assume that Hungarian-Canadian literature as an aesthetic phenomenon, as an art form in a modern sense, was created by more recent immigrants. The influx of thousands of educated people after World War II, especially after the revolution of 1956, secured the foundation for respected literary production, and provided a reading public which appreciated the work of the Hungarian-Canadian writers.

"Respected" is a word of considerable weight. How respected has Hungarian-Canadian literature proved to be? It should suffice to say that four of the most outstanding Hungarian poets of recent decades have been residents of Canada. They are: Ferenc Fáy (deceased in 1981), László Kemenes Géfin (now residing in The Netherlands), Tamás Tuz (deceased in 1992), and György Vitéz. Hungary, reluctant to recognize its authors living abroad, a decade ago gave considerable (although not unqualified) credit to these poets. Some of their works are also accessible to Canadian readers in English translation.

Prose writers and playwrights are generally not as well-known and recognized as poets. Similarly, it is not easy to familiarize the larger Canadian reading public with a popular prose that Hungarian-Canadian literature has developed from the journalistic essay, which claims to possess aesthetic quality.

How respected is the size of this production? I researched post-World-War II Hungarian-Canadian literature in 1980 and found that more than eighty Hungarian-Canadian writers had published literature in the Hungarian language during the preceding three decades. Altogether they produced 140 book-size volumes. In addition, there were numerous Hungarian-Canadian writers who chose to write in English. Everything considered, even without similar data from other Canadian cultural groups, we may safely say that Hungarian-Canadian literature developed rapidly and vigorously within a short time span.

Are Canadians familiar with Hungarian-Canadian literature? Perhaps to a moderate degree, or in general terms. But only if we take that segment of this literature into consideration which was either written in or translated into English. John Marlyn's *Under the Ribs of Death* is a Canadian classic, Stephen Vizinczey is well known, and the poems of Robert Zend or the second generation Nancy Toth, and the immigrant Eva Tihanyi, are occasionally mentioned in literary circles or publications. Otherwise, unfortunately, even scholars of Canadian literature or ethnohistory are unaware of the dimensions of Hungarian-Canadian literature.

One of the major difficulties is, of course, that other Canadian cultural groups also developed their literature in as many languages. As well, these literatures have not yet been assessed. Besides, Hungarian is not just another one of the languages; it is very different from virtually all others, and not spoken or understood by a great number of people. In Canada, only slightly more than 34,000 use it on a daily basis. A source of pride and joy for all Hungarians, their language has also been, in a sense, their destiny.

The present anthology is a welcome enterprise. While commemorating the 115th anniversary of Hungarian immigration to Canada, it also gives Canadian readers a representative picture of Hungarian-Canadian literature: its themes, styles, aspirations. The work presents the entire spectrum of a colourful culture with ancient roots. The reader will find not only the recognized masters but also the younger generation of authors and poets. Hungarian-Canadian literature is indeed in a state of constant renewal.

The editor has utilised the best translators available for the challenging task. Their skill, together with their understanding of an appreciation for Hungarian culture and language, guarantees that this valuable component of modern Canadian literature is presented in its full merits in this volume.

It is hoped that the reader will find this anthology rewarding in one additional respect: as a slice of contemporary multicultural Canada. At times this experience will be familiar, at times less so, or not at all. But, is this not what true literature is about?

University of Toronto

IVÁN BÉKY-HALÁSZ

An Irregular Sonnet

in the jungle of slogans and dogmas
you lost your way somewhere some time ago
now you want to escape although too late
in every liana you spot an enemy
boa constrictors watching you from above
lions' eyes burning in the darkness
lizards hanging from your shoulders
an army of ants attacking your loins
the survival kit went a long time ago
you eat roots you drink from footprints
mosquito bites bleed from your scratching

at home people knife each other
later they toast with red wine you want
to curse but your throat is swollen and sore

Like an Acrobat

Like an acrobat, who swings and glides
among the traps of treacherous trapezes,
missing the shiny iron of the bar,
to which the aim is safely to return;
so I'm swinging between life and death now,
below me space cruel and envious,
I missed my partner's waiting, trusty hand,
nothing will swing me upward any more.
Around the ring a deadly silence, fright;
the drums are rolling, reddish-yellow sand
is glittering in ever-changing light;

the leap has failed, there isn't any hope;
raise a redeeming net to rescue me,
catch in your arms my poor, plunging body!

Blessed Harbours

A ship put into the port yesterday.
She took on coal, water and canned food.
Dockers were swarming by thousands around,
agile conveyor belts and sluggish cranes.
Whistles, coal-dust and swearing thicken the air
At night the crew left on a shore-leave,
the pubs were noisy till dawn on the quay.

O women's laps, blessed harbours, where
I return to rest and where my desires
merry sailors go ashore to leave
with aching heads in the morning for
unknown havens, till the voyage ends,
where they won't weigh anchor anymore.

You see, such a harbour were you too, where
my desire took rest for a night, while
my ship loaded coal, water, food, though

the hangover still throbs here in my head.

Checkmate

At six o'clock the foreman went home.
The helpers collected the waste-boards,
the tools and the dropped U-straps.
At eight the moon emerged from behind
the clouds and began to play chess on

the two coloured, quadrangular network
of the scaffold. When I passed by
the blood was already strewn with sand
only the captured queen was still
sobbing in the darkness and a fallen
pawn adjusted his foot-clout.

It was not midnight yet . . .

JOSEPH CSINGER

Nirvana Grove

Like tall timber, I saw
the sweeping, dark, dense row
of your eyelashes grow
and myself shrink
to mere hallucination
flickering on the brink
of annihilation.

Lost in a redwood grove
of monstrous infatuation,
I felt them fall on me
in a wild chain-reaction,
lashing out link by link,
hair by hair, tree by tree,
triggered by a wink.

Skyline at Sunrise

The pushbutton impulse of
colossal greed suddenly
releases a wild growth of
skyscrapers: long switchblades
savagely knifing the surprised
morning in the abdomen.

Columbiad

(Columbus takes leave of America)

My dreams once read the map of your body.
Retracting slowly the lines of creation,
I reached your living shores with expectation,
cautiously circumnavigating your pleasant
peninsulas and scenic promontories,
unveiling from its jealous garment-waves
and lacy mists, the splendour of your shape,
seeking along your sweetly sweeping curves
the perfect place for a possible landfall
even if it could be my very last.

I sank the anchor of my heavy heart
in one of your intimate estuaries
to rest a while, until the northern ice
thawed off my wind-chilled bones
and cold numbed flesh.

Now, let my fingers and my fancy roam,
lost at will in the wild, exotic maze
of lush blond forest fires in your hair.
Please, do not smile, but let me taste a tear,
an orphan-drop from the Fountain of Youth.
Let me savour the salt of sea-blue eyes,
and all the fragrant spices of your Islands:
The consolation of your sunny south.
For I know well, I cannot keep for long
this newfound Eden's treasures to myself.
Discovering it, I lost Eldorado.

You can't remain a secret, and I know
that in the wake of my discovery,

you shall be ravished by a cruel breed
of young explorers, new conquistadors,
rapacious wild males burning all behind them,
to whom, since all is fair in love and war,
you shall give more in short, stormy embraces
than all I ever had. After the storm,
after the senseless plunder of your charms,
I shall not even be here anymore,
a crazy old man, to pick up the crumbs.

You send me back in chains, covered with shame,
to the drab, dark Old World, where I belong,
to die forgotten, poor, with no more hope
ever again to discover a New World.

I have outlived my time, die-hard Columbus.
The Seven Seas are wrinkled beggars' garments,
old rags, crawling with ships, as thick as lice.
No more miracles, no more sweet surprises
going beyond the borders of a smile.

There are no unknown, virgin continents
found by mistake: The Earth is fully Charted.

ROSE DANCS

Wild Boars Were Plundering the Corn

We were tiny tykes. We went to school from the most obscure village of historic Háromszék to Lisznyó, a place that happened to become bigger, as we grew diligently out of the grade school at Sepsimagyaros.

Every morning, five of us hiked across the Heveder, one little boy and four little girls, returning in the afternoon. In September, the farmers were well into their autumn work in the fields, so we had to travel by shanks' mare. The weather was relatively pleasant in October and in the winter we would be boarding at school, so our parents told us.

Oh, but we loved it. We were somebodies. As we slogged our way from one end of the village to the other, everyone regarded us with a glance. "Ah, so these are the scholars from Lisznyó," they would say to one another. "God grant you a good day!" we greeted everyone courteously, for which a curt "G'day" was the response. Then, after a couple of weeks went by since school started, the "G'd day" was followed by the question, "So, what's new down there?"

(The Heveder meant a climb whose lower incline ended in Lisznyó, so from the perspective of the Magyarosi folks, the village was down below.) "The same old things," we kept saying like grownups, for there was hardly anything remarkable going on.

Sometimes, there was sensational news, though. "Uncle Laci Damó had a stroke," we told Mr. Fanyó, the blacksmith. The news really scared the blacksmith, for he had a face as red as Mr. Damó's. The doctor from Uzon had told him he had high blood pressure due to all the bacon he ate. At another time aunt Gyertyánosi's only daughter was hit by a train in Bucharest, just as she was about to come and visit her mother. "Oh Lord, have mercy on my orphan soul," she keened under the Gang so loud that all the people ran out of their houses to hear what the moaning was all about.

It came about that we'd become the messengers between the two villages. Usually, when we got to the Oláh Hill somebody ran out from the field to the clay road to hear the news we gathered.

The women gave us apples and pears, sometimes even doughnuts to eat. Everyone subscribed to the daily paper published in Uzon, but delivery took place only once a week, sometimes even every two weeks. After all, the mailman was busy harvesting corn, or picking plums in his yard.

On October 15th we moved into the students' residence at Lisznyó. Thereafter, we could only go home on Saturdays, and Monday at dawn the parents took turns in driving us back to school.

My father had no horse, he could only harness our ox in the yoke, but uncle Joe, Ibike's father, thundered down the Heveder with us on the horse buggy. We almost gave up the ghost on the pitted, stony road, our spleen and tummy all shook up when he lashed between the horses with his horse-whip. But it was fun. The ride had shaken us awake by the time we arrived at school.

On the evening of October 23rd, two of the teachers supervising supper, the principal of the boarding school and the cook, aunt Adélka, began to whisper among themselves. One was more agitated than the other, and the cook responded by whining, "Oh, me God! Oh me God!" We didn't show much interest in whatever they were worrying about. They were too busy to notice that the order broke up at the tables and the restless ones drifted outside.

At bedtime we made a big commotion, but at ten o'clock we were expected to blow out the oil lamp, and go to sleep.

In the middle of the night I woke with a start to the wild barking of the village dogs. The pandemonium scared me. I reached over to the bed next to mine to wake up Ibike. Our hands met half way, as she was about to wake me up also. "What's going on?" I asked, my teeth chattering, but someone hushed me up. "Be quiet!" We could hear men talking outside.

"The alarm fires are burning all around," said a firm voice. "The towns Réty, Egerpatak and Bita lit up at dawn. Uzon replied a bit late, but they may have had to get rid of the militia first. Old Mr. Bordás has mentioned that, according to folks, the wild boar is plundering the corn. Fire scares the beast away, that's why they started lighting fires." I recognized the voice of András Zsigmond's father, as saying: "The wild boar, you say? I like that one. Let us agree then, fellows, that we all say the same thing if the militia becomes suspicious." "What about the others?" said a man impatiently, whose voice I couldn't recognize. My bed was closest to the hidden blind street, right next to the wall.

I could hear them talk and I was wondering why'd they speak so mysteriously? "The flames are up everywhere. I saw two of them flickering at the mountain top. Antal Berdi was the first one to give the signal. Patak is all right. At Magyaros, at Oldal, and on the Oláh Hill, but probably on Hegyfarka also somebody must have warned off Réty and Borosnyó. In Bikkfalva Mr. Harkó took things in hand."

"Watch out, somebody's coming," a choked voice said alarmingly. "Give me the storm lantern," said the Zsigmond-voice. "G-day," uttered some of them, followed by many more "G-days."

"So you've decided to come," said someone, while hands must have been shaken. Their answer sounded like, "Muk es meg," but I may have just imagined it so. I was falling asleep again, but I still remember wanting to sneak a look to see if the newcomers came from Magyaros and if my father was among them. Three days had gone by since I last saw my family, my parents and my little brother and my little sister.

It was an ordeal to get up in the morning and wash in ice-cold water, drawn directly from the well by the principal of the residence. There was some warm water, too, but only a mugful for everyone. We were asked to economize. Shivering, we stood in line in front of the building, waiting for breakfast. For breakfast we had cumin seed-soup with brown bread dunked into it. We spooned the thin soup feeling anxious and depressed – perhaps due to lack of sleep.

Or perhaps because aunt Adélka failed to greet us with a warm smile, something that we have become accustomed to as she doled out the food. She had also changed her usual blue polka-dot kerchief to a black one. This caused me worry and, while hurrying outside to line up for school bell I sidled up to her. "Has somebody died, aunt Adélka?" She glanced at me in wonderment and said, "Somebody may have, my child." It was a strange answer, but in the morning tumult I had no time to pay much attention to it. I was only twelve years old and the mysterious atmosphere of that early morning was soon forgotten.

As the windows had no drapes on, we had clear view of the street. It was a strange sight to see the village folk, men and women dressed in black.

During the first break we all gathered at the end of the yard. From the neigbour's garden a huge plum tree was leaning over, and as we saw aunt Julcsa, the owner, leaving the house, we rushed over for a bit of snacking. Somehow though, the plums had no flavour that day. That's when a girl, late for school, came up to us. "There's a revolution in Hungary," she said excitedly. "My mother told me so. But we're not supposed to talk about it." Since I was a well-read little know-it-all, I knew that there had already been a

revolution in Hungary, a hundred years before, when Sándor Petőfi, our great poet had vanished on the battle field.
But it sounded so very romantic, especially when I was
reading his patriotic and love poems in my mother's book of
verses. "Will it be the same this time, too?" "Hush," my
friend cautioned me. "Don't talk about it loud!"

In the afternoon my mother, along with a few other
mummies, came for a visit. "My darling, I had a chance to
come, so I thought I'd see how you're getting on. I'd also like
to have a word with some of your teachers," she said while
she re-braided my hair. "Mother, is it true?" I asked her.
"What? What're you talking about?" "The revolution. The
Hungarian revolution."

Suddenly she tightened her grip on my shoulder. "Oh,
it's true, my child, but let's not talk about it. It's not your
business. Not yet." Her voice was so sad, so tender that I
started to cry.

"Mother dear, I am so afraid." She said to me, still in
great sadness, "Don't be afraid, my precious. The good Lord
will not abandon you. And don't you worry, He will help
them, too," she said looking at the direction where the sun
was about to set.

"But we must hurry, it's getting dark already. I left the
little ones to your grandma," she said, while still caressing
me. "What about father? Couldn't he look after them?"
Grandma was busy enough running her household, looking
after four grown sons and grandpa and helping out on the
field as well. "Your father? Well, he is away for the day,"
replied my mother. "The wild boars are plundering the corn.
He is out there protecting the plot."

Once the mothers were gone, we came to realize that all
our fathers were spending the night on the field, chasing off
the wild boar. It sounded rather strange though, as quite a
few of them had already finished harvesting the corn.

"Maybe they're too scared doing it alone. It's much safer keeping the fire going in a group," opined Jancsika Kese.

And even after we've spent the whole weekend at home, the adult males were still away.

It was always the excuse of the wild boar. The men of Lisznyó were also gone, in search of the wild beast, taking along whole slabs of smoked bacon, pots of fresh plum jam, and sacks of flour. My girlfriend from Bikkfalva, Emmi Harkó, confided in me later that the men have gone to fight in the revolution. Since the Russians were threatening Hungary, our fathers took food stuff to feed the revolutionaries. Our Székely people in Transylvania are strong, they'll help them win the fight, too. "My godfather from Szacsva has also joined up with them," she said. Her remark was cryptic and needed elaboration, but all she said: "Don't pass it on to anyone."

Uncle Fam of Lisznyópatak was also out stalking wild boar, announced his son, Ferike, the six-grader. But by then we all knew the truth. As we weren't supposed to talk about it, the mystery made us so much more agitated.

In the cemetery, candles were lit two days before All Souls Day. The sky was overcast, twilight came early, the Nemere promised snow. We were not allowed to leave the students' residence after nightfall, so we looked at the beautifully illuminated mountain slope from the courtyard. My sweater was not warm enough, I was cold, even though my mother had knitted the wool good and thick. The candles burned for three nights, while black and white figures prostrated themselves over the chrysanthemum-covered graves; the women and old men stood in vigil. All around the Háromszék-basin, alarm fires engaged in silent conversation with the flickering flames of cemeteries, as if exchanging messages. On the weekend in the cemetery of Magyaros my mother and I prayed by the grave side of my great-grandparents. I wished I was allowed to bind my head in black cloth like grown women, but my mother waved me away. "Leave it, my darling, it's too soon for you," she said. Then she produced a black ribbon she had kept in her sewing box. "Put this in your pocket. The Good Lord'll notice it there. No one else needs to." We could see as far as Egerpatak. In the dull twilight some kind of mysterious power moved into the landscape. It appeared as if a common feeling, a communal will had clapsed together all the villages of lower Három-szék part of Transylvania, illuminated by flames of the dead and the living.

Sunday afternoon, we, children, ran to the outskirts of the village, shielded our eyes against the sun, staring into the distance, hoping that our fathers would return. And even though it was cold, we laid down and flattened our ears to the ground, listening for the sound of faraway. And we did hear it too! Not footsteps, but the rumbling of the earth.

Aunt Albina, the wiseacre of the village, maintained that it was the sound of the Russians invading Hungary, which made the earth weep. "How would you know that, Albina?" people inquired. "Never mind how, I know it," she said, lifting her apron to her face as if wiping sand out of her eyes. We did believe her. The radio! Let it be. It's better to leave the listeners in obscurity.

At long last the fathers had returned home. One by one they drifted in, exhausted, soiled and humiliated.

My father arrived on a Sunday. We greeted him with joy. He was weary and downhearted. He just sat there, tears running down his cheeks. I could hear his sobs from my room, while mother prepared warm water for him to wash and clean clothes to change.

"We couldn't get any further, Annuska," he told my mother. "The border guards ruffled us, the pigs threatened to shoot us. They made us dislodge our sacks, then waved us aside. One of them asked me, which one was mine? The striped one, I pointed at it. We could see across the border, Hungary was a stone's throw away." Father must have overcome by weeping, as I couldn't hear him talking through the closed door. And after a while he went on saying: "The soldier says, 'Make your choice, man! Will you go back home, where you belong, or I'll shoot you dead. Get a move on, or I'll do it, so help me. Leave your satchel and off with you.' He ordered us around with a malicious countenance on his face. Oh, Annuska, Annuska, how humiliating it is that we're such a bunch of cowards . . ."

It was heartbreaking to listen to my father, the courageous Székely, talking like that. As he kept on crying silently I covered my ears with a pillow, lest they realized that I could overhear them. I was also crying my heart out.

My schoolmates must have had similar experiences.

As we came to learn later on, the men from the Konya family have tried to cross the Hungarian border at the nearby town Érmihályfalva, but they were captured by the Roumanian security police lurking around in civilian clothes. First they suspected that the men were about to pay a visit to the local minister whom the police had already arrested and taken away. This pained us even more, as the priest in question was the Reverend Kálmán Sass, who had baptized me many years before.

I was born in 1944, when the frontline reached the city of Nagyvárad. My mother took refuge with me in a shelter during air raids. I was baptized in a dark shelter by the reverend Sass, so that I wouldn't perish a heathen, in case the cellar was hit by a bomb. My mother told me this story many times over after she moved us to the Székely region following the war.

Mr. Aladár Utõ was less fortunate than my father. He got back badly beaten up. The saying went that on the way home he was dead drunk, fell off the wagon and the horses stomped him badly. This, of course, was a barefaced lie, as uncle Aladár was not a drinking man. He had a brother living in Budapest and he was determined to go and look him up at all cost. As they had no children, he refused to turn back at the border. The militia men have turned him back all right, breaking three of his ribs and his nose. The latter stayed crooked for good.

I kept the black ribbon in my pocket for a long, long time. The earth kept rumbling well past Christmas in 1956.

Translated by Paul Gottlieb

TAMAS DOBOZY

Red Love

My immigrant grandmother bestowed her good drugs upon me just to show she loved me most. When I visited her I usually toked up strutting along the sidewalk to the hospital, blithe and clear as a gentlemanly stroller. Five months pregnant, my wife was processing our second child, like mail order. She said, I'm going to give you another child, like saying no refund. During the first pregnancy she stopped indulging in drinks and drugs during gestation. But the second one was an accident she didn't care to cherish. We stayed at the bar, swallowing grandmother's pills, falling over the furniture, giggling like little boys, waking the baby and then arguing – until my wife got too rotund to manipulate, then we called people over, watched videos and drank immaturely. We weren't as young as our friends, but nobody refereed us; most of them were my high school music students.

One day the schoolboard phoned me to say they'd found me unethical.

The next morning, I took a walkman to grandmother's bedside. Her three grandkids on a rotation: each of us came calling every three days. My brother, sister and I thought this the best schedule. That was the least company we'd have to keep her. We all had money to make, lives to work on.

I'd play Mascagni's intermezzo through the headphones to her on the deathbed. Too bad I smoked dope beforehand, because I might have understood the experience. The music delayed death for a couple hours more. She forgot all spectres. "The most beautiful night of my life," she said. "The most beautiful man." Her face, changed by the music, gave me the crawlies. But she just slammed death into its cupboard like a wooden monkey. She smiled at the night. "Good music can keep death slow," she said, in the mother tongue: Hungarian.

Like stories, my grandmother's life had high points, separated by decade long chasms. I'd say "climaxes" instead of "high points" but that suggests orgasms. Orgasms played no part in grandmother's life.

The intermezzo from Mascgani's *Cavalleria Rusticana* figured largely in granny's good times. You must understand what that piece of music represents. You can revile opera and still appreciate the piece. Scorcese did it best. I show my students *Raging Bull* and play the opening where DeNiro, bouncing on his toes, warms up in the boxing ring. Imagine it: boing, boing, up and down, fists jabbing in slowmo, while the auditorium roils silently around, a black and white mulch of cigar chomping bitches and frail bastards with umbrellas. But DeNiro blinks their funny faces away. What concerns the boxer also concerned – no joke – Mascagni when he dredged the only piece of genius in his mediocre soul: the fighter (in this case, grandmother) alone in the ring is at once adversary and defender.

Sometimes you hold your own hand. Sometimes you punch yourself in the mouth.

"How's Milly, István?"

"Milly's good," I said, "the last time I saw her."

"And the baby?"

My grandmother didn't know about the second pregnancy. "Nagyi," I'd say, "do you think I could borrow some more of those pills? I still have that pain in my neck."

The farce in your neck, her expression as much as said. "I don't have any more. I gave them all to you before."

I got up, started rummaging in her bathroom's cabinet, spilling containers into the sink, checking them anyhow. I usually jammed anything fun into my pockets, but the prescriptions that day gave no hope. If only my students could have seen me. I was sweating. "There's nothing there," she yelled. "You took it all last time." I came out before the nurses heard her. Then she started telling her love story.

Piling my body into a chair, holding it hurtfully straight, I wondered if the government had a program for people like me, and why I wasn't on it; not that I minded relying on the old notion of family ties.

Grandmother began.

"I loved my adultery. The church let me separate but no divorce. You know why I left your grandfather? Because of his sins. Not making enough, hitting me, taking food from my children, being selfish. Such a boring man in bed! But I never made love to anyone else. No. No place to go except in alleys on the lids of garbage cans and I wasn't raised in the military mansions of Vienna to act like a prostitute. I never made love to my *cavaliers*."

"Dudes," I said to her, "call them dudes please. Are you sure you don't have any more drugs?"

"The doctor is a Jew," she said. "You know how Jews are."

"You racist Austrian!" I smothered the anger. "I'm sorry, Nagyi."

"I'm not an Austrian!" she screeched.

"Sure you are. You were born in Vienna."

"Capital of the Austro-Hungarian empire! My parents were both Hungarian. You don't know how big a Hungarian I am!"

"Okay, okay, don't get excited, Nagyi." Anything to extract even the smallest dosage out of her. "Go on."

She went, as usual, into the highlight of the highlights – with factual overtones.

"He was like a Hungarian Errol Flynn."

"Don't you mean Rudy Valentino, Nagyi?"

"Too girlie," she said tartly. "Errol Flynn was man enough to not be a homosexual on screen."

"What do you mean? Man enough!" I got indignant again.

"Just shut up and listen," she said, not wanting to get into another argument that would end with her comparing contemporary society to the Roman Empire in decline.

The guy looked like Errol Flynn. The kind of man who refused to be photographed unless he could put one foot up on a chair and lean forward, both arms on the knee. A hardware store of white teeth.

He'd married long before. My grandmother and he met in cafes or echoing train stations. They'd clasp, kiss and blab their private feelings. He had eau de cologne. She managed a bath. The conductor in the background, red hat and armband the only colour around. A local busker, head pointing down, grating a favourite on the fiddle strings.

They were introduced in her workplace. He was inspecting it for some communist council. Delving into their political integrity. From the gold of his tie clip, she could tell he was into socialism for the bucks. Everyone in the office greeted him affably, but Nagyi refused to shake the Soviet puppet's hand. He kissed her on each cheek anyhow, saying: "From each according to his means to each according to her needs." Then he haughtily walked off. Hate purred inside Nagyi.

My grandmother slept on her desk some nights. Her

mother looked after the four children. She got paid extra for overtime and always accepted the hours. The forms, their duplicates, the carbons, and ledgers made splendid bedding. She had a beat up crucifix in her pocket.

One of the kids caught a cold that worsened seriously. The doctors told her only a caustic mixture of honey and lemon juice would scrape the phlegm from her daughter's windpipe. At that time, Hungary didn't have any honey or lemons among its commodities. She wept to the drivers working at the transport company. The next day she woke to a pot of honey between her legs.

"Those whole-hearted proles!" she said, still astounded.

I snapped back from examining her night table drawer, clean even of residue. "Oh yeah?"

She shook her head. "I can't help you, István."

"The story," I said, gripping the ends of my shirtsleeves and pulling them down.

"What's wrong? Something with work? Milly?"

"Just go on with it!" I shouted, hunkering down in the chair again.

There were two lemons as well. A tag on them which said: *Marxism is the opiate of the working class (but tell anyone I said that I'll deny it)*. "Normally I wouldn't have taken anything from him. But anything, anything for my children."

She could build him from sound. That's my metaphor. But she said his leather soles pattered in a distinguished way, and from that sound she guessed the shape of his feet, the roundness of ankles, thin, bone-fronted shins, thick thighs, cock, gut, chest, neck, head. So she materialised him from the floor up with her back turned, by relying on sound over sight. Spinning away from him she stripped everything off as it had gone on, until his footsteps faded away.

But they kept being on the same streets.

After she took the lemons the debt owed became a relationship. The nurses mixed the honey and lemon juice, heated them over low flame and spoon-fed it to her daughter. The syrup scoured out the phlegm. Grandmother started saying hello to him. Going out to lunch.

The schoolboard wanted to see me for "fraternising" with the students. So they saw me. Then they gave me a hearing.

"Your present wife was once a student of yours, wasn't she?" the vice-principal asked me. She jotted down my aswer, paused, amended her shorthand, read it to herself. Then she looked at me, pushed the frame of her glasses up her nose, and said: "We are aware of the date on the marriage certificate and when she dropped out." She wrinkled her nose. "Just as we are aware of allegations circulating when she was still your pupil." The vice-principal did not note my next response. "We are aware," she went on, changing the subject, "that, since your employment here, you have been arrested, but not charged, for narcotics-related activities, once concerning trafficking . . . Yes, I know. The point is that two of those 'supposed' arrests were in the company of present and former students of yours. Now," she folded her hands and the committee leaned forward with her, "we have a reputation . . ."

They wanted to see me again today. I decided to go to grandmother's and get the kind of aid that comes first.

"He took me to his home one night," Grandmother sighed. On the balcony he took a silver whistle from his pocket and blew it without a sound. The dogs in the street, for miles, wouldn't let up barking.

"A real master of the pack," I snickered, checking my watch, noting the hour between now and soon. "I don't have all day, dear Nagyi," my words saccharine.

"What's the rush?"

"I have an appointment."

"Why are you so sweaty?"

"I'm hot." I sound like talking lard. She can hear every-thing even with Mascgani crashing through the earphones. "Can't you help me?"

"He was dignified but not a snob," she says.

He could drink. Drink it all. In fact, he slammed pálinka with a half-gypsy lounge pianist and holocaust survivor called Rudy. After one such night he went home, took one of his wife's furs, showed up at my grandmother's place, tears in eyes, promising a divorce. She told him he'd wake the children. "Go home. Don't make love to your wife," she instructed. He promised and walked home, placing his dress shoes in one wheel rut on the road. The mink coat the party had confiscated and redistributed from the former elite dangled off his arm.

"His wife was human too," grandmother says, reaching forward to put her hand on my forehead. "You have a fever. Milly doesn't cook well. Not like me."

"Milly orders fine food, Nagyi, I mean cooks . . ."

She shook her head. "He told me his wife fed him grapes on their honeymoon in the Bulgarian resort. Seedless grapes," she intones, "a delicacy! She was too human to know you pay for subservience twice," my grandmother pontificated. "I hated that woman."

I pull her hand off my forehead. "Please Nagyi? I prom-ise I'll listen to the whole story if you give me something now."

"I didn't kiss him back for months."

She let him slobber his lips over hers, sloppily for someone so debonair, but didn't help him make it. "Return my mouth to me," he told her one night along Andrássy boulevard, beside the neo-classical mansions of an era consigned to ideological quarantine. So she kissed him right. He whispered afterwards: *"Workers of the world unite!"*

Coming to and from work passer-by's stared at her. Not cowed by notions of secret police surveillance, she twirled every time someone in a black suit with a notepad went past. She'd heard of Siberia. The guys in trenchcoats kept copying down their notes. Often those certain footsteps approached, only to waver off when government agent lookalikes were around. But his footsteps always returned, closer each time.

They offered her a promotion if she joined the party. She told them she couldn't miss Sunday mass. They decreased her pay, put some incompetent in the position meant for her. She didn't help her blacklisting by standing at a compulsory workers' meeting, after the boss proclaimed Communism the peak of human accomplishment, and asking: "If it's the peak then how come the Austrians live better than we do?" She left to find other labour.

"Stinking Slav atheists," she said.

I raised my eyes to the heavens, my body waxy as a side of bacon. "Are you sure? Haven't they prescribed marijuana for your glaucoma?"

"No. You're sick, István." She leaned forward and took my fallen hand. "You have to get better. You have to stop."

I drag my hand to my chest. "I have problems, Nagyi."

"I have a pill," she says, raising a capsule between her thumb and forefinger, into my light.

I prepare to pounce.

"No, no, no," she stutters, distraught for me. "What am I doing?"

"Tell me the rest of the story," I whisper – the shrewd extortion.

Red wine gave him red, itchy bumps under the armpits.

He kept drinking anyhow. Not only depressed from lack of consummation but because the higher-ups had "accidentally" put him on a list of questionable softies, whose number had increased, threatening the party and state. He didn't know who'd labelled him but he signed everything – every retraction, every oath, every character assassination against his colleagues – hoping for reprieve. He and Rudy wallowed in sorrow the night the party notified him of their concerns for his health, of their suggestion he go to Russia for medical treatment. Rudy sat down by the piano and played *Claire de Lune*. Such decadent music had been forbidden, but now, with the verdict, who cared? "No more of that fucking Shostakovich," he told Rudy. The two of them laughed until Rudy, grabbing the bottle by the neck, broke it over the piano keys. Red wine seeped between the ivories.

"When's your flight?" Rudy asked. But Errol Flynn put on his hat and lurched out.

He had tickets to *Cavalleria Rusticana* that night on Margit's Island. My grandmother found him morose at the pickup but didn't ask. The opera happaned in an outdoor theatre. The crowd flexed and wobbled, a million tuxedos and gowns. As the Easter Chorus came on she snuggled under his tense arm and they floated, his cheek against her head.

During the intermezzo two men appeared in the isle and whispered something to Errol Flynn, who was nodding before they finished. The two agents went out before them. He took grandmother by the arm to the back of the theatre, told her to go home and good-bye. "Why?" my grandmother asked, totally naive.

"I've been recalled by the state. I'm politically defective. They're going to take my health into their own hands."

She put her arm around him. "It was me, wasn't it? You tell them this for me," she said. "Will you?" He nodded. "Bread and lard are not equitable with happiness."

The intermezzo played and she grabbed for him. A minute of their time went past.

"I wish I could have made love just once," he said. "I guess we didn't have the means."

"Or the needs," she replied.

"I left in 1956," she said, rolling the pill in her palm, almost hypnotising me. "Some of us were leftover Nazis, some Orthodox Christians, some of us just plain."

Some who beat their wives, I thought, some who slapped their husbands, some who kept daddy's little girls and mommy's little boys – nobody unblemished or devine. "Were there even dissidents named Igor?" I asked her, eager to humour the old lady.

"We baked someone a birthday cake after we got over the border," she said.

"Nagyi," I frantically tilted my watch, "I have to go in two minutes."

"I know. I won't go into it." She looked out the window, one face in an appendix to the anti-Communist martyrology, a book whose main pages are compiled with those who stayed to die, strewn with lips that defied, limbs that didn't goosebump at threats, resolute brain matter.

"They're all dead," she affirmed.

Then she took the pill, held it out, and pushed it down into my outstretched tongue.

ALEX DOMOKOS

The Prisoners' Gift

The Caucasus is like a great East-West wall leaning on the south end of the Ukrainian prairie. It is the only armour against the arctic wind. On the northern side of the mountain, the wind unloads all the gifts she carried from the North Pole, covering the whole area with deep snow and ice.

Georgiewsk was one of the many P.O.W. camps in the Northern Caucasus. I was one of the two thousand inhabitants of that camp in late November of 1947.

The camp, enclosed behind barbed wire, seemed deserted. Tracks in the snow and thin smoke columns were the only signs of life. Life? It could be characterized in three words: cold, hunger, and weariness. Even under these circumstances there were some people who could maintain the best aspect of human character, the will to help.

The barracks were dug into the soil and the snow-covered tops looked like a big graveyard. Our barrack was twenty yards long and six yards wide. On one side were the stairs, and on the opposite was the fireplace. In the middle, between the log-built bunks, was the corridor of communication. Two frames with glass eyes placed in the ceiling provided the necessary light. During the winter it was essential that some self-made candles should be used to break through the darkness. The earthen walls were always damp, and the air was full of smoke, but we had long ago lost our sense of cleanliness. Ragged clothing, wooden-soled shoes, one underwear change monthly, baths few and far between, and the never changed strawsacks, led to philosophical apathy.

Life focused around the meal. The tension of constant

hunger was lessened for a while only at mealtime. That was a time of relative happiness. The food was gulped down with remarkable speed, and then we were waiting again, like addicts for a drug. Everybody found it necessary to do something to distract his attention from the irritation of hunger. Many of us played chess. Some mended clothes or carved wood with endless patience, but most sought the oblivion of sleep.

One of the officers, who had been a P.O.W. in the First World War, said, "The war prison is nothing but waiting between meals." As time passed we understood better and better the meaning of his words.

In the last days of November, many labourers were frostbitten, so the Russians allowed us to stay in the barracks. Even the workshop labourers were not forced to work because of a wood shortage. So it happened that Béla and I, who were both working in the cabinetmaker's shop as wood-carvers, were sitting on my bunk playing chess. More accurately, we were looking at the board while our nerves were keyed for the signal, the bell that preceded the soup distribution.

Béla was older than I. He was around thirty-five, of medium height, stoutly built and dark-haired, with thick mustache. His home had been in Transylvania. I was glad to work with him, because he was a master of the chisel. He was easily angered but a good comrade.

"Your move. Why are you taking so long?" said Béla.

"Yes I know, but don't rush me. I have to think it over," I replied. Both of us were irritated by hunger.

"I'll go to the hospital this afternoon to see Steve," said Béla, and added a friendly invitation. "Are you not coming?"

"I certainly shall. Poor fellow."

Steve Révész was also a Transylvanian. So was my wife.

Everything in connection with my wife's home was dear to me. We had been married only two months when I fell into the Russians' hands. I kept close friendship with the Transylvanian boys. Steve was a quiet young man, a teacher by profession who was not used to hard physical labour. But when the snow fell and the wood shortage became urgent, our masters forced us to go into the forest to fetch logs for the camp. These marches took place once a week. The last one had been too much for Steve. He sat down on a log in the forest and fell asleep. The guards noticed the missing prisoner only on the way home, and went back with dogs. He regained consciousness in the hospital.

"The doctor says one of his legs must be amputated," murmured Béla, at the same time giving me a checkmate.

"Could it not be saved?" I asked.

"No. The leg is lifeless. The only question is whether they could cut it under or above the knee. Dr. Gereben wants to cut under the knee so Steve will be able to use a prosthesis. Otherwise he will be a complete cripple." Béla frowned as he spoke.

"And the Russian doctor wants to cut above the knee?" I asked.

"Yes. It is less risky and simpler," he said. "If the lower cut is unsuccessful, it must be cut above the knee anyway. Why should he work twice?" Béla observed wryly.

"This is the radical way of thinking. Why take chances?" I said.

"They don't care too much about the fate of a P.O.W., but I hope that Dr. Gereben can do something about it," Béla said. "We must go to see the doctor."

The door opened and we saw two men carrying the barrel with the soup. The interior was filled with steam, making the whole place resemble an ancient shrine. Silence fell over us. Everybody ate with concentration. The smallest bit of bread and the last drop of soup were eaten carefully. Béla wiped his mustache and rolled the Pravda paper into a cigarette, filling it with "mahorka," which looks like wood-flour. Then he gave me the tobacco and paper.

"Here, have a smoke."

I rolled the cigarette. We smoked, enjoying the rough flavour of the mahorka. We disposed of it only when our fingers burned.

"Let's go," Béla said.

The hospital was about 200 yards away. It was a real building made out of sunbaked bricks, whitewashed inside. Inside it was warm, and there was no smoke, just the smell of burning spruce. The place had real iron beds with relatively clean bedding. It was luxury. Naturally it was a privilege even to work in the hospital. The orderlies and doctors were not paid, but they did enjoy unlimited food, clean underwear, a bath and the pleasure of not working in the cold. We stayed in the waiting room, which was not really a room, just a square, partitioned off.

"Who are you looking for?" asked the orderly.

"We would like to see Lieutenant Révész."

"He's asleep. We can't wake him up."

"Of course. But at least we would like to talk to Dr. Gereben."

"Wait here a minute. I'll call him," said the orderly, and went.

"He's a fat boy," explained Béla jealously.

"They sure have plenty to eat, and they do only light work. No wonder that they are ready to kiss the Russians' boot just to stay here," I said.

Dr. Gereben appeared so we stopped the conversation.

"Are you Lieutenant Révész's friends?"

"Yes, doctor. We would like to know what's going to happen to him," Béla explained.

"The right leg must be amputated. Tomorrow Major Starinoff will perform the operation. I'll assist him."

"Above the knee?"

Dr. Gereben nodded.

"For God's sake, doctor, why not take a chance? Must that young man become a complete cripple? Is this your way of assisting?" Béla cried.

"It's the Major's order," the doctor replied. "I'm only a P.O.W. Just like yourselves.

"Doctor, as a P.O.W. you must obey, but what about your oath as a physician? Why don't you protest?" argued Béla insistently.

The doctor shrugged. "I've tried everything. Major Starinoff is my superior and he does not argue with ethics."

We stood dumb and slowly turned away from the hospital. I could see that the doctor's face was pale and expressionless.

The dark comes early in winter time. When we arrived back at the barracks, the candles were already burning. Somebody had put a wreath above the fireplace. It was approaching Christmas. It was good not to be able to see the future and foresee the four more Christmasses that were to be endured in camp.

The next morning, news of a scandal shocked the camp. A man came from the kitchen, excitedly announcing, "Doctor Gereben has carried out the operation on Révész during the night. He cut off the leg under the knee at his own risk. The Russian major expelled him from the hospital, and he'll have to go on construction work. But if Révész's condition turns for the worse, Major Starinoff has threatend to court marshal Dr. Gereben."

For long days this was the issue. When we came back from the shop or the others from the construction, the first question was, "How's he?"

In the meantime, Doctor Gereben worked on construction. His face became thinner by the day. The orderly whom we met in the hospital had also been expelled because he had voluntarily assisted Dr. Gereben with the operation. When we recognized him we felt guilty.

After four days, Steve's condition improved. Even Major Starinoff admitted it. He allowed Dr. Gereben to return to work in the hospital.

We were barely into December, but our attention turned toward the oncoming Christmas. We celebrated. Such is human nature. We were busily cleaning and reparing our clothes and decorating the barracks walls with evergreen branches. Only Béla did not participate in the preparation. He was silent and disinterested.

"What's the matter, Béla? Something is bothering you."

He inhaled smoke before he answered.

"You're damn right. I feel ashamed. See those people, Gereben and the orderly? They did something for Steve, while I, a close friend, did nothing. After what those two did, it seems so inadaquate to give him a carved cigarette box for Christmas. But what else can be done?"

I understood his feeling because I felt the same way. What else could we do? He has enough to eat in the hospital.

"Maybe we could make him a pair of carved crutches," I suggested.

"Don't be a fool. But wait, we could carve him a leg! An artificial limb. A prosthesis!" Béla shouted.

We got all excited about the project. We went to see Dr.

Gereben. He sympathised with us perfectly and he prepared us a sketch. The next day he provided us with the proper measurements.

Only then did we realize how difficult it was to make an artificial leg. It was a combined effort, involving some sewing by the tailor, a lot of leather work by the shoemaker, some metal work by the smith, and the carving by us.

Everybody was enthusiastic. We coordinated the plan and made exact timetables. We had twelve working days before Christmas, not much time under such circumstances. The smiths worked from the skeleton of a rusty tank, the shoemakers had to use the half-rotten boots of the army, and we looked for two days to find the proper light, dry wood. Determination conquered all the difficulties.

Doctor Gereben gave his instructions. The woodframe must be movable at the ankle. The leather work must fit perfectly in order not to cut off the blood circulation. The metal frame must be strong but light, and flexible at the knee. These were serious tasks to be filled. Now all of us felt that if we didn't make this prosthesis, our Christmas would be so much poorer. We worried about the condition of Steve's leg.

"Will it be healed enough to wear it?" we asked.

"Yes, that's the idea. A surprise for Christmas."

The last night we worked until midnight on the exactness of the joints. Then Christmas day came. About four o'clock in the afternoon the doctor went to the hospital with the prosthesis. We P.O.W.'s formed a semicircle before the entrance. Some of us held spruce branches in our hands. Somebody started singing "Silent Night." The song was taken over by all of us. As we sang, the doctor opened the door and Steve came out leaning on the doctor's shoulder, both his legs moving. We burst out in a cheer.

I glanced at Béla, and even with the tears in his eyes, his

countenance told me beyond all doubt that his desires for Christmas had been fulfilled.

Translated by the author

CSABA DÓSA

High Jump Competition Sometime in 1970

The elements cease to exist, their fury subsides
the clamour ceases, the throbbing does not interfere.
At this stage the only time that exists
could be held in the palm of our hand
and the earth with its total weight sticks to my feet.
There is no pretense in the poem now for that would
     distract,
no horseplay of raw forces, no playful moods,
no invocation, no supplication to the gods,
a deep breath is only a faint message in the wrinkles of the
     bloodstream.
I bow my head – deep silence in the stands.
Could imagination be transmitted to matter?
That's what we're waiting for, hence the curious crowd.
My tinkering, which they see as mastery, is only a ruse
to postpone the final outcome.
In my excitement I am flooded with ideas
Icarus flexes his muscles but after a while desists
since beyond a certain point the figures don't matter
he is moreover wholly composed, with the utmost assurance
he spreads his arms
his torso becomes a statue cast in bronze
shoulder blades touching in intricate swordplay –
     everything in its place
his face brushed by a breeze-like smile – Oh, the leather
     sandals,
Yorgos the Cypriot's perfect craftsmanship.
Every step he takes reaffirms the perfect concord
of the muscles and the delicately compressed energy.

There must be a master craftsman somewhere who knew
     that the client
was waiting for the perfect footwear
while he prepared himself for the task folding in two
the finest Zebu hides
merchandise smuggled from Phoenicia, two layers interlaced
to make the sole pliant, resilient, scented leather
fashioned not for marching but for running
not for retreating but for pursuing,
matter attempting to pursue imagination.
Yogos had somehow sensed this, it is as if
in one the sandals he stitched his right eye,
in the other his left ear.
He agreed because his simple being sensed it
in the way Icarus gave his instructions.
He too will be the bearer of the secret
though untouched by the crowd's hysteria for he knew
the secret is vulnerable.
But, more curious than he was humble, Yorgos wanted
to witness and hear of the performance of the "best sandal
in that land already reached by galleons."

Icarus stands by the quay in tense restraint
Yorgos by the breakwater awaits
the arrival of the smuggled merchandise,
the finest Zebu hide the galleons carried
and wax, ebony, ivory, the highly strung vulture,
these are what Icarus waited for by the quay and nothing
was missing from the list.
For obsession cannot bear anything to be lacking
anticipation so impregnates imagination
that matter itself is affected, the fibres excited,
the organs, the pampered inner entities which in turn spur
     on
the imagination, where perfection is for everything

the function in perfect order:
for at any excess beyond this state of perfection the organs
     revolt.
The imagination seizes this marvellous chance for perfect
     balance.
Which one? In Yorgos curiosity was dissolving.
You alone will know when heart, liver, pancreas
are set in motion and the electrons cut into
the underbelly of the torpid brain. There is only one chance
to escape: get rid of the shackles.
Yorgos was smiling with an accomplice's smile:
I shall see your secret and hear it as well.
He tilted his hat at a rakish angle to hide
his face's lack of eloquence.

I am testing the surface of this turf, the product
of far-reaching scientific research, my trusty sneakers
were custom-made by good old Lajos Szatmári
whom I rewarded with two dozen Wilkinson blades.
I secretly double check the sneakers – did he really sew
     his eye and his ear into them? He didn't, he put in cleats,
the talons of an eagle: perhaps he doesn't believe
in myths any more or is he more humble than to
interfere rudely with others' aspirations?
True, we live now in different times, he will be allowed
to be part of the crowd, wearing his wire-rimmed
     spectacles
unlike the one-eyed Yorgos.
The one-eyed sandal able to leap miles at a time
sticks to the rocky ground like a magnet to iron ore.
Icarus rubbed the wax on his limbs and embraced the bird,
as I ran my fingers through Agatha's hair they took root in
     her scalp,
like a huge bird she bent over me, wings spread
tailfeathers spread.

You were the missing part of my dream, whispered Icarus.
The eagle let out a screech as though on its wings
it balanced a storm. I'll take you away
in the heated wax of my burning body. The eagle has struck
spreading his thighs, the talons immersed in the wax,
        drawing blood
I must take something with me, you have robbed me of
        something;
there is no winner and no defeated.
Agatha's face relaxes, she is calm and beautiful and she
        stands there naked
facing the eagle-like Icarus in his feathers fit for a warrior.
Before take-off I touch Agatha's breast – it helps me relax.
I must be relaxed or else my moves will be rigid.

As I lift my head up a few hissing sounds are heard in the
        stands:
these are the fans – they at least know what is about to
        happen,
for them the result does not matter.
The beauty of motion is all that counts though this isn't
        really
what the whole thing is about
for matter is only imagination's slave.
What gifts will the slave receive from his master today?

I wish you had stayed with me,
Icarus, embrace me once more

                :I can't do it, I can't
                I must make the journey
                for the sake of my own peace of mind
Will you come again?
Will you return to me?
                :Of course I will, just as soon

as I learn the devotion to heights.

The sandals holding firm to the bare surface of the Greek
    soil,
the cleats ripping loose gravel.
One more step, I am extending my stride to get closer to
    take-off
so doing, the last stride falls somewhat shorter, creates a
    tremendous
surge for momentum
everything the momentum at its peak, in a flash I shall be
    lifted up,
Icarus airborne. He circles above the abyss, spits into the
    sea below
with piety in his face, his head thrust backward
he is scaling the hights.
The body emerges, the spectators ignite, the body at this
    point
in a state of weightlessness,
that desired split second when the body can free itself
from the letters of gravity.
Look – a hundred thousand really believe this to be
    possible.
I clear the weight with ease. Below the foam rubber
    cushions, the green lagoon.
Agatha awaits me with sinking heart, the spectators roar
    "Higher! Higher!
Show us what you can do . . . go higher!" No,
I have finished for the day!

Let Icarus glide on his own for one more day.

English version by Christopher Levenson, with Peter Kaslik

GEORGE FALUDY

Sonnet 86

As yet I have said nothing of my nursery.
It has always been my belief that the windows,
the stone balcony with the raven's nest,
the mirror wherein dwelt the little boy

The old peddlar made of cracks in the ceiling
above my bed, my teddy bear with the messy
mouth (from time to time I fed him porridge),
and the wolves lurking beyond the shutters . . .

never disappeared like the rest of my past
but remain there still, in the bombed-out house,
and may still be seen should you walk through,

along with the little boy in the mirror, the teddy bear,
and everything else there that holds out in silence
against the vicious wash of time.

English version by John Robert Colombo

62 Birbeck Road, London, N.

This is the tiny house in which we live;
the furniture is battered, second-hand,
but everywhere we turn are books; it is
enough to have the liberty to read on,
content to learn, to be alive, to be,
and yet not be possessed by our possessions.

London, 1961

English version by Robin Skelton

IBN *Amar Al-Andalusi, A.D. 1000*

The parks, the nights, the naked bodies' blur,
the fountains, and the library of course,
the olive trees, and the minarets, the myrrh,
the honeyed scent of joy without remorse.
He had a fair sword and a jet-black horse.
In pride he wrote this, because it was clear
that all within the high walls of Seville
worshipped and quoted him, the Grand Vizier:

"I am Amar. The fame of my verse flies
over mountains and the western sea
and from the south and desert wind replies
only a fool is ignorant of me.
A golden lizard on a golden disc,
if I slither from the lewd lips of a boy
in the eager ear of an odalisque
she leaves her master and becomes my toy.
Nor will this change after my body lies
under my obelisk."

He was cheerful and happier than I
for when on Spanish domes the arabesque
loosened and fell, he never questioned why,
or why people grew flabby and grotesque,
and did not sense the fabric's fading dye
or in his own tunic the broken thread,
the fountains of the city running dry,
he did not taste the filth inside his bread
or see the boys who knew his poems die
or view the burning library with dread.
Brave and clever, he failed to note the fact

that faith's no help, nor wit, courage, or dagger
that no philosophy will resurrect
a culture, once it collapses forever.
   Spain, Summer 1974

                              Translated by George Jonas

Death of a Chleuch Dancer

(Chleuch dancers are dancing boys of the Chleuch tribe in
   Morocco, who are famous for being stained blue)

I burst into the marketplace
in time to see his face. It was sulphur-yellow.
They were lifting him from the ground, for he was dead;
the lover he'd cheated on
had murdered him. Now two men were holding the killer,
three kicked him, and one came behind with the dagger.
The crowd began to follow.
And I was left alone beside the blood, which
did not penetrate the dust, but lay and rippled.
And I called back many gentle words the dancer had
      spoken.
I remembered the smell of his body, wild honey it was.
And I thought of his bright blue hair, a banner and
pillow at night.
How should I
honour his bittersweet memory?
I sat in the dust, destroyed, beside his blood,
and beat the flies away.

                              English version by Dennis Lee

Sonnet 89

More and more shadow fills our rooms:
high-rises, towers, office-blocks
loom newly up, year upon year,
shutting out pale blue sky, all loathsome.

These bird cages of hard blue steel
are to become our death's memorials
when winds alone are the sirens of Toronto
and her streets. No matter. Wave your hand

in greeting now, for in our pots the flowers
bud and bloom still in their many colours,
each one of them aware how much they mean

and how much they are loved as pigeons wander
tiptoed on our windowsills each morning,
tapping upon the glass to be let in.

English version by Robin Skelton

ENDRE FARKAS

Old Country Talk

You said it
or maybe me
                it doesn't matter who
one of us did declare that

There are times
               like always
when we feel as if
we are immigrants in ourselves

Why we left Where
we do not know

and even if we did
there is no choice about arriving

We are given a threadbare shape
into which we slip
as into second-hand silence

and come into this country
this perfect empty place
with used suitcases & lungs
full of foreign languages to be forgotten

the one here
is accented by fur & fire

A Valentine Poem
For Elias Letelier-Ruz

A flick of the switch
and the current flows

The lights come on
The radios play love songs

I think of you
an exile poet
who because of the flick of a switch
and the current that followed
can not sleep
can not have children
can not sing a love

Poem
(for Ken Norris)

'Twas the night before Xmas
and all through the land
the children were sleeping,
the lights were enchanting
and the gifts were all wrapped
and waiting under the trees

And like so many others
I curled into easy chair
to stare into the snap, crackle fire
and waited for the vision

But nothing was revealed
so I turned on the news
and watched the world unfold

I watched fly-freckled children
dying of starvation;
lots of starvation;
lots of close-ups
which made for good T.V.,
followed by a report of the world's generous response
followed by a report of a gory train bombing
followed by a commercial break

The images flicker back and forth
between tragedies and little miracles
and close with a human interest story from the Holy Land
where thousands can get a room at the Holiday Inns
and hundreds of sharpshooters line the roofs of Bethlehem

FERENC FÁY

Towards Fifty
(For István Vas)

Slowly the expanse of your life closes.
Under your fine, tiger-striped brow
– as your eyes open on blood and death –
the desert wind herds in
the moss-green shadows of fear.
You live darkly, between blue silence and dust;
and, in the cool dawn, lap water
from the victorious hoofprints of young bucks.
The earth thrashed you. Crunching
memory's bones, you gnaw the shreds
of antelope-days benumbed in death,
their graceful motion a dream rotting,
tasteless and soft as mould between your teeth.

Only yesterday the sky trembled at your voice
and great waters shivered far off;
the curved moon's brass-scissored scorpion
struck at you – weeping clouds fled . . .
and bursting from dry trees
the condor-stars scattered in a yellow scream.
. . . Today the land sickens at your smell
and vomits you from its mouth. You stand
in the night, the neck of your days
noosed by copulating shadows
and ringed teeth grown against you.
You would kill . . . but can only scratch
in the dust for decaying words – scraps buried
from yesterday's plenty – and you know

you have been left alone with your death.

Translated by George Payerle and Karl Sandor

Spring Hymn

I am your shadow . . . I am your dust.
Above me, with the flame-edged iron
of your plough,
you turn the fields' loam-heavy life.

Only my nails still grow, and my hair;
a tornado spins in my lap;
in the riverbed of my mouth, shoreless,
its whirlpool drinks your showers.

You tore away my lacy fingers
and crushed my pillowed tongue . . .
Lord, how to touch you now?
Lord, how to praise you now?

And your worms suck me;
the tangles of your root-world;
in my heart your mildewed silence
opens velvet petals.

Only lava and cinders bubble
from the caved-in wells of my eyes.
On your world's dark roads
I thirst to see you.

Snakes chain my feet;
with cool mud you sealed my ears . . .
In the realms of your shining world,

Lord, you live, but without me.

Dig deeper, only don't sunder yet
the bone arcades of my skull and ribs.
Let me bear
the burdens of your light world:

of the poor, the peasants
on your good earth-warm,
plough-scored-
who shine now
in the glory of your face.

Translated by George Payerle and Karl Sandor

Flood

The tree tumbled to the foot of the hill
and asked to eat. – But not a single bird
brought food.

The tower reached out an open hand . . .
the man kicked at it . . . and sat
by its burning light, to keep warm.

There was no bird!

An ancient fox drifted through the fog,
hunger like sulphur yellow on his gums;
with the two-holed flute of a chicken beak
he piped to the cackling winds,
and the moon dried on his forking eyebrows.

Then my trusted teeth fell out
and from the scary, stinking cavern of my mouth
troubled thoughts peered with bright
owl eyes at the evenings' gusty warmth.
On my alkali tongue, God built a fire
from sticks of my windstrewn words
and spitted his bone-rack life for roasting.

There was silence, but I needed to sing.
They besieged me with the fetters of the dead,
the hobble of desire, the noosed reason of my past
. . . and the deep-urned flower of my aloneness
blossomed into a yellow star on my chest.

I feared; but blew my big clarinet:
brave reed of the new times
hammered into my sphincter-tight days
that I might blow to the fugitive sky
with all the force of my cornmush-fuelled wind
bawling yipeeyiay
for the merrygoround joys of man.

The maimed world surrounded me
and in its delirious din
spat my clumsy songs about
like the husks of pumpkin seeds,
blind to the small corral of word and spirit
where my lovely, tethered dead
grazed the grassfires of parched-out dreams.

Filth overwhelmed the dam of my words
and flooded out my precious phantoms' refuge.
. . . trees swell, grass weeps, tiny villages spin . . .
The torrent hurls me over
and in my weedy eyes

man-deep darkness lies in wait
for mosquitoes.

There's no air. Coppery froth boils in the abyss.
The fox whines, the tower spins with me . . .

But out on the bank a willow starts to run.
Before everything can drown into grey
it reaches after me and catches hold my hand.

Translated by George Payerle and Karl Sandor

PAUL GOTTLIEB

The Phase-Out Man

As a child in Hungary, I was attracted by a lottery advertisement, stating "every second ticket wins." I walked into the store and asked for second ticket. So much for win-win and generating extra wealth without anyone losing anything.

I had tried to explain win-win to the laboratory staff of Lanotex, the largest state-owned lanolin and cream factory Ildiko has just bought. The factory produced cheap and quite adequate baby cream, soothing a million bottoms a year, producing hundreds of thousands of pounds of the stuff. More than that, they sold every single jar and tube they manufactured. Trouble was, every time they sold one, the state, which owned the factory, lost about twenty cents.

This happy state of affairs would have gone on forever, except for the Berlin wall coming tumbling down. Within a couple of years, Lanotex was competing in the free market. And holding its market share, thank you very much. Except for one small problem. They kept losing money at the same rate as before. So the near bankrupt state decided to stop subsidizing inefficiency or whatever it was that kept them losing money, and put Lanotex on the the block.

My friend and patroness, Ildiko MacRoberts, a formidable combination of Hungarian dash and Scottish shrewdness inherited from her late husband, was the smartest investment manager this side of Warren Buffet, came in with the winning offer. She took Lanotex off the hands of the government. In short order, the decision was made to raise the price of the product to profitable levels. Which meant tripling the price of this trouble-soothing commodity. The factory people allowed themselves a sigh of relief, the mothers of

Hungary protested as the cheap goo disappeared from the stores. At the same time, well-known western brands appeared on the shelves. They cost slightly more than the Lanotex ointments, but were handsomely packaged, nicely perfumed and charmingly advertised.

Soon, Lanotex was losing even more money. Which is when Ildiko made the deal she planned to make in the first place. She persuaded the makers of the well-known western brand to buy Lanotex at a good price, and produce their own brand in Hungary. This is when I had to go in the country and explain that the laboratory, research and quality control departments had to be cut down, the labour force halved, because new, automated American machinery was coming in. And that wasn't all the good news. Those employees who would be retained stood to receive a substantial raise.

Those found redundant would be compensated from a special fund we had negotiated with the buyer, which would pay a generous severance of two weeks of salary for every year worked at Lanotex. It was a win-win situation, no losers. The state had its burden lifted, the factory was saved, the product will be a success, employees get a raise. Those found redundant would get a new lease on life, enough money to help them find a better situation, or set up their own businesses. The new owner would help with counselling, offer free courses in enterpreneurship, marketing and sales, resume writing, personal hygiene and grooming, the lot. Everybody wins.

The chief engineer, a woman, came into my temporary office afterwards. She had to be let go, her salary was among the highest, and the western owner wanted to have an American in charge.

"It's not about me," she said before sitting down in the chair across my desk. She wore a white lab-coat and her head was covered in a white turban, like all the female employees at Lanotex.

I waited.

"Do you actually believe what you've been telling us?"

We were speaking in Hungarian. Her expression radiated a sad kind of contempt. Her eyes were a beautiful golden hazel and they bore into me unblinkingly. She seemed to be in her mid-forties, but as it turned out, I guessed wrong.

She put me on the spot. The woman, her name was Agnes, Dr. Agnes Detre, knew I was raised in Hungary.

And that, she must have felt, precluded hypocrisy. Hungarians willingly betray each other to foreign powers, and have done so throughout their history, but hypocrisy is considered by them an English sin. They prefer to be brutally, honestly dishonest, when necessary or when an opportunity compels them. If a Hungarian does you harm, he will immediately blame you for creating the situation in which he or she was forced to do you dirt.

"Did you actually believe what the Communists had been telling you for almost forty years?"

Answering a question with a question is a good, sound rhetorical device in Eastern Europe. They blame it on Jewish influences.

"Are you no better than the Communists?"

Another question upon a question.

"I plead the fifth," I said, deciding that there'd be no further questions.

"What does that mean?" This time, her question was warranted.

"I decline to answer on the grounds that I may incriminate myself."

"Oh yes," she softened slightly. "I saw the movie."

Then her hard stare returned.

"What you're telling me is that you've been lying."

"Not at all. Truth is relative."

"Not where I come from," was Agnes' fiery reply.

"Dr. Detre, remember, I spring from this soil myself. Truth has always been highly relative here. I've learnt my resume writing skills in this country when every year I had to twist or change one fact or another. And I was still in my teens when I left. I love this country, but it isn't a fountain of truth."

I suddenly realized I was far more deliberate, even brutal, than I usually am with women. She was damn attractive, in a way only Hungarian women can be. Tough and vulnerable at the same time.

She radiated contempt, but the pursing of her lips showed as much come-on as righteous indignation.

"Why don't you give me a straightforward answer?"

"Because I am on duty. My professional code of ethics does not permit me to drink alcoholic beverages and give straightforward answers."

For the first time she smiled. She worked at suppressing it, but then she must have told herself, what the hell, the man's answer wasn't half bad.

She tilted her head sideways. An auburn lock escaped from under the white turban. It seemed dyed. But the colour suited her.

"If you want a straightforward answer, we must leave the premises. I'll pick you up at the staff entrance in ten minutes. I'm driving a blue Renault."

"I am driving a red Opel."

"Point." I conceded. "So why don't we meet for a drink at the Anna Bar?"

"Too many tourists and mafia," she said.

"Game," I sighed.

"How about the other side of the river which is where I live. The Budagyöngye. Do you know where it is?"

"Set," I said.

She gave a girlish giggle.

"Match?"

"Match."

We parked our cars side by side, arriving at the same time.

We sat down at a sidewalk table. At a snail's pace, a bored-looking girl sauntered towards us, and asked for our orders in the flattest monotone I've ever heard. The espresso-bar was quite empty.

Most people were still at work, but we were free as birds. I was a consultant and she had just been fired.

Agnes ordered an espresso and a cognac. I asked for the same.

"Do you still want my answer?" I began.

"Yes," she made a tiny, funny grimace. "Er . . . what was the question?"

"Why do you keep answering questions with questions?"

"Why indeed?"

We both burst out laughing. It was an easy laugh. The lukewarm spring afternoon sunshine glowed through the smog and haze, and gave her auburn hair, now freely cascading, a halo of sparks.

"If I remember correctly . . . "

"Do you think you can remember correctly?" Again the tilt of the head, now with the addition of her fingers raking her hair, her right arm, behind the nape of her neck, exposing shaved armpits and the smooth fall of her short-sleeved blouse.

This was being too obvious. I'd been away from Sandra for three months, so I was becoming more than susceptible to anything feminine, but this was an unexpected onslaught. Had she not cancelled her visit, Sandra would have been here with me just now, possibly saving me from what seemed more and more inevitable.

And, quite frankly, irresistible.

Her most recent letter, announcing the cancellation, more or less bluntly suggested that we separate. So, I could, I suppose, turn fully Hungarian and blame the victim, if that's what Sandra had become.

I was getting angry. Sandra was still under my skin.

"Yes, I can remember. Still. My mind's not completely out of control. Not yet."

"That's very impressive," she said and lowered her arm. No sense in wasting more energy at this stage of the game. She regarded me with a mixture of frost and bemusement.

"But I'm fast losing it," I added, taking my attitude down a peg. "Here it comes. Do I believe any of what I've been saying to you. Right?"

"Right," she smirked.

The coffee and cognac arrived.

We stirred our coffees, I took a sip of cognac. She downed half of hers.

"It's a matter of interpretation," I conceded.

"Is this how you operate in America?" she asked, "trying

to convince people that losing their jobs is for their own good?"

"Sometimes. Other times we say that 'this is hurting me more than it hurts you.'"

"Hypocrites."

"Why, of course. But it sounds true at the time."

"Well, mister, here in this little country we're past masters at it. We've been fed outrageous lies for decades, pretended to believe them, and went about our business."

"Which was?"

"Survival."

"How are you going to survive," I asked, and I think my voice betrayed a measure of guilt.

"It's not your problem, is it?"

"What if it is becoming my problem?"

"Then get lost. I don't need charity. Especially not from the enemy."

"Am I the enemy?"

She regarded me up and down. She nodded slowly.

"I'm beginning to think so."

"And how do you treat the enemy in this country?"

"As if you didn't know your East European history. We sleep with them."

"Must be the reason why Hungary attracts enemies. Too damn sexy."

"Why, thank you."

This was to be difficult, but I am unable to change.

"I am married. Sort of."

"I am sort of married too."

"My wife is in Canada. We are thinking of separating."

"My ex-husband is at home with our daughter."

"Baby-sitting?"

"No. He's never left. The apartment shortage. You seem to live separately from your wife, but somehow you're still together. I am together with my husband, but we're completely separated. Interesting."

"We're Canadians. We have a desire to separate but fear the consequences. It's at the heart of our politics, too."

"Please don't bore me with politics."

"I have a decent enough apartment across the bridge."

"I am sure we'll end up there eventually. Order me another cognac."

I must have looked at her somewhat quizzically. She shook her auburn mane in a huff.

"I am not a drinker. It just relaxes me and helps me fake orgasms."

We drove separately to my apartment on the Pest side of Budapest.

In springtime at dusk something takes place on that side of the city that comes on imperceptibly, something I have never seen anywhere else. The long streets and boulevards are lined with plane trees, horse chestnuts and linden, and suddenly you realize that thousands of sparrows have descended on the trees, covering every branch, like dark fruit, and begin a continuous, shrill, high-pitched chirping that lasts until the sun sinks below the rooftops. It's not a particularly pleasant sound, it's more like an alarm warning the city of the darkness to come.

My Budapest apartment was in an old building, high-ceilinged, with french doors overlooking the street, two rooms, a kitchen and all modern conveniences, including a Hungarian-made portable washing machine in the bathroom, which took off in the spin-cycle and performed a throbbing can-can dancing as far from its original position as its electric leash allowed. It was the subject of cabaret jokes, and even figured in an avant-garde erotic film.

Like most appliances in Hungary produced under communism, it was ungainly, noisy, overbuilt and quite reliable, once you figured out how it works.

We entered the room off the vestibule and I took the light raincoat off Agnes's shoulders. Her breasts eagerly crushed against me as I turned her around. Our long kiss, thanks to the cognac, tasted warm and plummy.

Hand in hand, we moved slowly towards the bedroom, our bodies becoming more and more familiar to the touch on the way.

The wooden slats of the blinds were stuck in their tracks. We could be seen from across the street. But I had an idea I've learned in outdoor theatres. I turned on the bright floor-lamp and aimed it at the window. It gave us enough reflected light so we could see each other, and it blinded anyone who would want to watch.

She took off her blouse and I began to fumble with her bra.

"Don't." She said. "Not yet."

I cupped her breast in my hand and began to explore her with kisses.

"How old do you think I am?" she whispered.

I'd figured her to be in her mid-forties. But to be on the safe side, I thought I should say thirty five. Then, in a moment of inspiration I said, "You could be my daughter. About twenty-nine?"

"You sweet, lying man. I am thirty six."

A strange thing about women in Eastern Europe. They are haggard and look more mature than their years. But they seem to become better lovers and more interesting to be with as they get older. Maybe only at my age. But I somehow don't think so. The writer who made the title, *In Praise of Older Women* a catch-phrase around the world, is a Hungarian.

Afterwards, lying in bed, she lit a cigarette. She offered it to me, but as a reformed ex-smoker, I wouldn't try. But I enjoyed her second-hand smoke.

I put my lips to her ears and stage-whispered. "If this is how you fake an orgasm, I'd like to be there for the real thing."

She smiled sweetly, but with enough ambiguity so as not to spoil me, and rewarded me with a long, smoky kiss.

"Enemies," she said.

MARIA GREEN

Of Birds and Jews

I was just pondering upon the ambivalent nature of the human heart, when a strangely-shaped crooked tree flashed upon my vision. Suddenly, through association of ideas, a sharp and precise visual memory unfolded itself full of life, colour, shapes, smell, and warmth, escaping from the depths of my very being where it had been long submerged. The key image, the crooked tree, revived the aura of my youth.

In *Remembrance of Things Past,* Proust compares the subconscious memory to a Japanese toy. The children fill a bowl with water, steep in it little crumbs of paper, previously without character or form. Immediately on absorption, they expand, bend, take on colour and shape, are transformed into flowers, birds, people, and castles.

In such fashion, the magic wand of the crooked tree expanded, took on the colour and shape of an earlier time in my life. I found myself in T—, in the castle of Count T— during the last year of the war.

Lunchtime. Thirteen people sat around the huge table. I, the tutor, was at the end of the table, with my young pupil. The topic of conversation was, as usual, the weather. Not in the English sense, stating the obvious, that the day was pleasant or the weather inclement, but in the peasant way, overlaid with superstitious connotation. For such people it is safer to complain about the weather than praise it. My suburban background had, at first, precluded my under-standing of the rules of this game; and therefore when T— complained about the rain one day, and the next day proved to be radiant, I had, at first, commented joyfully upon it, lauding its beneficial effect upon vineyards. Automatically they would intone their litany: "Yes, yes, but the millet! The oats! They need rain." When it rained, the obverse applied and dire foreboding was uttered about the vintage for that year. Finally I learned enough to amuse myself by anticipating the order of their comments; when I proved to be right, I was filled with elation, like making a good move in chess.

On exhausting the first topic, I looked forward eagerly to the next – horses and horseracing. The genealogy of the horses dovetailed neatly into a third topic: the detailed analysis of the family trees of recently wed or defunct fellow-aristocrats. There was yet another topic: the most important of all, which, through the engendering of strong emotions, seemed of fitting climax to the prolonged orthodox ceremony of lunch. Probably the needed anger to stimulate their stomach acids after a rich meal. This fourth topic was subject to delay.

To digress momentarily into a vignette apropos of what later transpires, Schopenhauer, dining in a small restaurant, would always put a gold coin on the table at the beginning of the meal and then sweep it into his pocket at the end. One day, the waiter could no longer contain his curiosity and asked the meaning of this odd procedure. "It's simple," was the answer. "I promise to give this coin to the first beggar whom I encounter, if one day the English people at the next table do not discuss horses, dogs, hunting, and the weather." I, like Schopenhauer, was just about to remove my imaginary gold coin from the table when an unusual event occurred, which further delayed the fourth conversational gambit.

It was a grim winter day and a biting wind swept over the prairies. Suddenly a little sparrow from a gnawed tree plummeted frozen to the ground before the dining room window. The countess cried: "Look at the poor darling!" and all heads turned instantly towards the grotesquely twisted little body in the snow. The countess turned to my pupil, and rolling her r's in the aristocratic fashion said: "Fetch the bird, my dear." Everybody half-rose from his chair to watch the girl rushing toward the little hunchback in the snow. I did not move. Sitting in cloaked indifference, I was astonished to observe the countess's eyes filled suddenly with tears. A feeling of guilt enveloped me. I keenly felt my indifference amidst this display of compassion, my inability to shed tears over a dead bird. The countess tried to revive the little body with the warmth of her breath but failed. She tossed the corpse into the ashes of the fireplace. Her moment of compassion was gone.

Finally broaching the habitual fourth topic, she turned toward the priest, and with tears not yet dried, announced: "Never shall I forgive Hitler, never, for doing such a poor job. All the Jews and all their children should be exterminated."

She was commenting on the decree which had been published in the daily newspaper that children whose blood was gentile as well as Jewish would be spared in Hungary. The priest cast a meaningful glance at the countess and solemnly declared: "Ausradieren!" (This was the term Hitler had employed to describe the "blitz" of Coventry.) Eleven people picked up the concise implication of the priest and went on liturgically: "Ausradieren, that is the solution!"

I was prompted to wonder then, as I do now, how cruelty and compassion can, in Janus-fashion, dwell side by side in the human heart.

TAMÁS HAJÓS

Breaking Up

I was late again
you waited 20-25 minutes
irritably walking up and down
in the late afternoon dusk
between the clock and the flower shop

Of course I could have said
transportation was terrible
I was held up by an old acquaintance
I had to wait somewhere for someone
I could not leave in time
because of this and that and therefore
I could have said
to avoid
another quarrel

When the coarse contours
of figures and the cityscape
were pieced from the darkness
only by the neon sign's glow
when noises withered to a rustle
and drowned in the silence of the night
shortly after
I paid the bill
and we left the cigarette fumes
of our caustic argument
in the coffee bar
shortly after that
your clinging embrace
fell cuffed aside

among the blood-shadows of squat houses

Translated by George Payerle, with the author

Morning

Rows of sleepless nights
push you awake into morning's
unaccustomable torture.
Today's buses and streetcars roar and clang
without you toward the offices and factories,
a segmented flood irresistibly pouring.

Strange old narrow streets: agitation, exhilaration.
From the gardens of brightly painted houses
(like faces of middle-aged women)
the fresh taste of morning breaks out
and overwhelms you.
How quickly
the gateways of cool, armpit-odoured tenements
can be forgotten.

This is the day
that takes you in hand and crowns you.
O how much youthful belief, how much conflagration –
O how often have you asked yourself
when your way has stripped off your soles:
Who helped till now? Who waited?

Translated by Joaquin Kuhn

Partway

Why does the loaf lie still unsliced?
The detached modulation of the mind
splits the silence,
the vocal chord snaps obligingly,
and only habit sustains
our withered glance from fainting away.

Why does the room lack warmth?
Nobody cloaks the shadows.
The mouldering furniture is mute,
while a forlorn sigh
torments itself into mere exhalation.
And partway, light congeals.

Translated by Joaquin Kuhn

GEORGE JONAS

Bridges on the Danube

1.
It takes much time to gain a little ground.

For instance, at the gateway to the Chain Bridge
the stone lions and I
have tried to out-stare each other for years
and now I may be winning.

2.
The Margaret Bridge
looks as it did a few seconds before
a German demolition crew (by accident)
blew it sky-high
                    some years ago.

At the time
a yellow streetcar took off gracefully
achieved an altitude of forty feet
circled the river gently
                    then it made
a spectacular landing.

Now I'm waiting hopefully again
as a new yellow streetcar crawls across
the reconstructed bridge, but it doesn't
repeat the performance.
                    Maybe next time.

Nocturnal

Oh how we entered
      dear madame dear
a temple well tempered
      oh how we entered.
Glances held four beats full
slim fingers sculptured slim
icons with stained
gestures newly painted
cool nipples textured cool
all centres centered:
            lean
invisible man: keen
woman, heads turning slowly, in
we went, skin
brushing against skin,
      oh how we entered, a drop
at a time, a stop
after each note
a flute
in his crushed velvet suit
a harp,
strings taught in her smart
Missoni coat
      but now a little fear
      strikes the hammerklavier
where, how much, through what jumbles,
snakes, bones, trinkets, truth-serums, iron maidens,
whose nails
across whose eye
for that matter how soon or why:
Perhaps a lapse
perhaps a lapse again, perhaps a lie?
      Dear madame dear

with all centres centered
how well tempered
        is the temple we entered?
Now for a last brilliant passage
slim fingers on the keyboard of her spine
his eyes crushed velvet blue
        c'est tout.

Six Stanzas on Homesickness

The Tower thought that I was alone
And placed himself squarely before me:
"Now what do you do?" he said
Happy, that I was not amused.

"I am with my friends," I murmured,
"Tower go away, go away.
You mean nothing to them at all.
This is something purely personal."

I closed my eyes, not that it helped.
"Tell them about me," the Tower sat down.
I was embarrassed for who would care
To bore his new friends with an old Tower.

"We were children together," I blushed.
"I can't turn him out, can I?" I whispered.
Unbidden shadows crossed the room
My friends looked at me with some concern.

"His first stones were laid in the tenth century,
He really is an interesting old tower,
I saw him every day, going to school.
Maybe he has something important to tell."

But my apologies were all in vain
My friends' eyes grew cold and seemed to turn inward
And I thought Towers must mean more than friends
But then he left quietly, I never saw him since.

JUDITH KALMAN

The New World

Along crescent streets muffled in snow, zipper-hooded adventurers emerged to plod past the split-levels whose rooflines had oddly descended. Overnight the snow had risen, obliterating the primary hues of doorways, and filling the undeveloped fields with a crystalline blankness that felt like the start of the world. Nylon snow suits crackled as our buckled boots broke trails to the park that joined our crescents. Children were first to venture out into that white sea that frothed over our boot tops. Station wagons stayed landlocked in carports. Businesses, like adults, stalled, opened late. Shovels came out after we were already in our seats, socks damp inside buffed leather. Puddles formed in lockers. By lunchtime we could spring home on firm treads left by sidewalk plows, and crunch up the walks shoveled clear by fathers before they'd left for work. But in the opening bars of those winter preludes we sounded the first notes. We children of morning in the new world. A world pure in its erasure of woods and pasture, where even the rutted earth that would fill in the spring with pools spawning tadpoles was a transitional ecosystem; promising streets that were newer yet than those bordered by saplings that matched us in height; streets as obliquely connecting, navigable only by automobile and bicycle and humming happily with the mechanical whirs of an emerging world.

I had fallen in love with the newness of Ville d'Anjou. I loved the shape of the houses, spare and oblique. I loved their colours. I loved the playground and its futuristic apparatus. The painted bars of the rocket ship that, last summer, I was still afraid to climb to the top. The clean sand. The amoeba-shaped wading pool painted aqua like the sky. I adopted this landscape, having come from a world that history had disfavoured. Like a false start, it shouldn't have happened. My place now was among the split-levels, bungalows, and duplexes of Ville d'Anjou – a world without war or want or fear – on the eastern edge of Montreal. The last inhabitable outpost before the island's desert stretch of refineries. A glimpse of the future sliced from farmers' fields, and nestled like a spare-edged brilliant inside a baroque setting. The East End's characteristically dark brick facades were heavily curtained with evergreens. Spiral two-story staircases, curling with black grillwork, twined up the fronts of pre-war walk-ups. We had to negotiate those dark streets like a journey through the past before breathing a lighter ether once we turned north from Sherbrooke Street and climbed – not uphill, there was no grade, though I could feel myself lift – into a largesse of land and air, yes more air, the homes hardly impinged on the sky. I exhaled once we reached Chenier Street after the march of duplexes from Sherbrooke. On Chenier the bungalows began, and the ranch-styles low and sprawling.

In those tidy, self-contained domiciles, children knelt on wall-to-wall carpeting, watching electric trains rock around a track. Little girls hauled about blond-haired dolls as tall as themselves, pulling a ring on the neck to hear words in English. Their dinners, absurdly premature, were at four in the afternoon when my mother was lying exhausted, feet up in the lazy-boy. Their bedtimes were punishingly early when in our house we were still eating well not from a box. I didn't envy them. But there was something certain in the heavy hang of a thick and perfect ringlet suspended from a plaid ribbon. A location in time and place. A privilege in knowing trends, and a luxury in caring about them. I hankered for the sureness of these gestures. Inside picture windows young-looking mothers stayed home and dangled legs beside telephone tables. I loved this vision of ease and belonging. Living rooms were off limits when you stepped in after school. A glimpse of perfect composure like unblemished face. My family's duplex was new, but branded with economic expedience, a paying tenant and the proximities of shared walls. It set me apart, as did my older parents, and working mother, and empty garage.

On winter mornings my father was long gone on his trek by public transport to a downtown office, our front walk a crisp scar in the white expanse that had filled overnight, and the sidewalk in front a smooth swath to the neighbour's invisible border. He wouldn't let my mother risk climbing over snow banks to the street where, he hoped, at least a car or two would have left a track for her to walk in, for my mother, like me, had to make it in time for the schoolyard bell. She'd leave before me, giving herself extra minutes because the snowfall would slow her down, to be ready to greet her class at the kindergarten entrance. I noticed her pointy-toed boot prints and made my blunt-nosed marks beside them.

Dire threats of penicillin injections had impressed me with the need to dress properly for the cold: not only hat but scarf, not just jacket, also sweater. Two pairs of mittens, for one was bound to get wet. Sometimes, during her exams, my sister would be home to lock the door behind me. More often she left early with my father for her class at McGill. I locked the door with the key that hung like a charm under my cotton school blouse, and went out with the other children, into the snow.

My over-swaddled burliness made each step an extra effort as I waded through the wet snow on Boulevard de la Loire. Rounding the corner onto Croissy Circle, I took in a sudden, frigid draft of air. Immediately, it was not my hand that felt burrowed in the quilted lining of a nylon pocket; it was my hand grasped inside someone's larger woollen mitten. It came upon me like that. Like breath. Memory entered with cold air. I was working my way through the deep snow behind an early-century tenement. My sister's hand firmly clasping mine, and tugging me up the white hill looming largely ahead. My sister the school-going-age I was now. My sister big to my small. Our woollen jackets heavy with wet snow. The prickly leggings bunched between our legs rubbed thickly together. My panting breath behind the scarf a wet, thready steam forming an icy crust that grazed my nostrils. Trudging up, up, plodding sweatily in the cold. I followed my sister anywhere. Going up. Hurtling down. I assumed unquestioningly some good reason for our labour in that whiteness.

I recalled this scene often and others that were too dear to let go, even though they put me out of step with my new, untarnished world that had razed what came before. Eventually time took the life from the remembrances and framed them. Shuffling them over and over until their edges frayed. I brought them with me everywhere. Through each move, I sorted and shuffled, losing some inevitably in all the handling, so I never again had a full set and ultimately there were just a handful left. I have few memories of Hungary.

In my child-mind everything was alive, vivid and concurrent. To remember was actually to feel it. In Ville d'Anjou, on the fifteen-minute walk to school through snow up to my kneecaps, hot with effort under my nylon zippers, snot crystallizing on the scarf over my mouth, and snow stinging, not yet wet, as it bit over my boot tops, I remembered. Not in pictures, nor snapshots, nor narrative, but through the physical fact of being in two worlds at once.

The Budapest flat was long and sprawling. For a little one, it was endless. Along the floorboards worn so smooth I had only to watch out for the rugs with rough naps. If I slipped

and slid on them, I'd get something red and sore. Some of
the rugs were soft, though, and thin with age. They'd turn
up and bunch and trip me if I wasn't carefull. The rugs were
islands with their own landmarks. The raised bristly whorls
at the centre of the one by the kitchen. I liked to sit on it in
my warm felt pants and pat the horsehair surface gingerly.
See how I could tame it? Along the brown river of a hallway,
there were archipelagoes of throw-about worlds. I saw my
mother take them and shake them, and hang them out the
window sometimes. She would try to rearrange them, but I
made sure they found their right spots at last. The thick
woolly tassels combed neat and flat.

The brown river parted for doorways, some always
closed to me. "Karcsi's room. Stay out," said my mother,
then to my sister: "Close Karcsi's door, before the baby finds
his fiddle." And doors I wouldn't want to open, ever. The
one with the great roaring thing that shook and rattled while
it regurgitated water with terrible rushing force.

On weekends Apu came home. His tread on the landing
was our mother's cue to pull off her apron and tug her
sweater smooth. There would be sweets if I foraged deep
enough into the big coat's pockets. And the course rub of
thick arms around me. Skin loose and tender as held my face
to his. I thought I smelled the animals on his coat. He talked
about cattle, pigs, but it was just the soft musky fur of its
lining, sweetened by the smell of him. Karcsi would come
out of his room to shake hands, and would be asked to join
us for dinner although in any case he ate with us most nights
as part of his lodging, and his place was always set on the
diningroom table.

We celebrated Christmas like everyone else so we
wouldn't seem too different being Jews. The big flat surpris-
ingly close with warm aromas and flickering lights. Evening
lamps glowing. Up on the deep ledge above the diningroom

doorframe three small fir trees glistened with pink marzipan bells. I was allowed to finger them lightly when someone held me up. If it was a visitor, we were given a taste. The hard sugar coating glazed before it melted on my tongue. Pink, soundless bells, though their sugar hard like crystal made me imagine a little tinkling. I would gaze up from the floor, feeling sated.

The clapping made me startle. Who was this? Who was coming? The grownup voices knowing and festive. Mikulás. Look. Look. Like a big brown bear. His great coat turned inside out to show the furry lining, and a white pillowcase over his shoulder. What? Who is it? Mikulás. Your Apuka. Look, silly, what is there in his sack?

My first memory was heat. I saw it. Waves of heat dancing. Later I imagined a small room with a black stove. I put red flames into the picture, flickering behind a grill. But I knew the image first through my pores. A pulsing reddish glow I ingested with each breath and sigh of my tiny, growing body. The long rambling flat was difficult to heat during the coal shortage in 1954. Karcsi the boarder had a separate stove in his room, so that was the room my mother took for the new baby. Karcsi moved out on the divan. At dawn he met the coal cars pulling into the freight yard and paid the black market prices for which my father had left him money. His musician's fingers clasped on a sack of coal that by breakfast he let slide beside the nursery furnace.

My sister came in to warm up. She stood first by the stove, and looked into the cradle at me. If my mother was lying nursing me on the bed, she nestled her brief length along the curve of our mother's spine, and took strands of our mother's long hair, twisting them around her finger. I remember heat, a dance of gold shadows.

Out in the country, on the state farms, my father trudged over crusty fields to inspect livestock. Wide hands thrust into the deep pockets of his great fur-lined coat, he spun dreams of spring crops and fall yields. Trusting implicitly that his family was safe and warm and unbeholden. How did he do that? Assume decency. My father anticipated decency in others before he would suspect anything else. Decency in others when, after he had to leave his first wife and their child for labour service in 1945, they disappeared with every other member of his family, in smoke. When I was born, Karcsi the lodger gave up his bed, and my father entrusted him with all that he had.

We have a photo taken in Canada when Karcsi came on tour with the Budapest Symphony. He looks young in the picture. I am six and spilling leggily from my father's lap. We're all sitting together on the sofa smiling into Karcsi's tripod-mounted camera.

From behind there came a shattering of glass. It was a sound like day, clear and explosive. In the halls, apartment doors swung open, and from all of them people ran, spilling into the stairwell. My heart thrilled hopefully. Such excitement. My little blue double-breasted coat had been buttoned on me; there must have been time for that, but not time enough to lead me by the hand. I was tucked like a loaf under my father's arm while we bounced down urgently. My sister's able legs just a flick of white ankle socks in leather lace-ups as they flew away below me. My mother wearing her warm coat that flapped open as she hurried suitcases in both hands. Sun poured down with us right to the basement.

Inside was a camp. Bundles. Families spread on blankets. Food unwrapped, passed from hand to hand. From outside a deep rumble and vibration, distant and stirring. "Boom-boom!" I clapped gleefully. But my sister's hands covered her ears, and her face froze yellow as she hissed, "Shut up, idiot!"

Later I learned a name for the campout in the basement. It was the Revolution. That was still all right. A revolution, I was assured, wasn't a real war. War was when Jews were pulled from their homes and burned in ovens. This was only a revolution; we weren't the targets. Everyone in the tenement, Catholics, Jews, regular Hungarians called Communists, seemed equally afraid.

How long did we stay in the dim, densely-bodied basement? Three days? Two weeks? I took it in, learned it, and absorbed it like everything new. It became part of me. It must have had its rhythms that I turned into rituals. It must have been assimilable.

I remember most the closeness among bodies, having to step over and through the personal effects of strangers. A general mistrust between neigbours. Faces swivelling at the unexpected sounds, apprehension their common feature.

In the mid-morning hush of a city that had been punctuated by burns of gunfire and shattering glass, my father slipped through a slice of light admitted by the basement entrance. They went out that day for the first time, men mostly, slipping tentatively through the fragment of light to forage a few facts that might let us know what had happened. No one knew who was the enemy. And the Russians might mistake anyone for an insurgent. Russians were always feared. But that day it seemed quiet enough, possibly safe to investigate.

It felt strange, the grownup men gone. Almost like an everyday when the men went to work. We were left as usual, the children with the women, only they seemed uncertain. My mother had held Apu back for a moment before he left, as though she had changed her mind about letting him go.

When the door flung inwards throwing in the harsh daylight, when the light burst in on us, it was as much an assault, that brilliant flare, as the bereted silhouette that followed. The severe light seemed to radiate from the khaki-clad figure who had booted in the door and held his rifle out front. He waved his rifle at us as though we might hurt him. A sudden stillness seized all of us in the basement. Still, like when confronted with an animal in the wild, don't move, must not alarm it. Ha! I would have laughed another time; maybe before the basement, it would have been funny. Afraid of us children and our mothers cowering in the dark.

"*Jól van itt minden?*" Hungarian. Someone dared to answer, so perhaps a Hungarian soldier was not so bad. "Yes," a woman close to the door whispered. "Yes, all right. Everything here is fine." He tipped his beret – a peacetime courtesy – and, relieved to withdraw without incident, ducked back-first through the door, his rifle the last out.

I remember my mother's voice still shrill many months later during my parents' arguments and endless speculations. Insisting she wasn't going to cringe like that again. When that soldier had burst in and we didn't know who or what he was, which would be better, Hungarian or Russian, neither was good if he carried a weapon. All we were aware of was our own pitiful dread. She wasn't going to cringe like that again. Enough! She had been through Auschwitz, now this. She wasn't going to raise her children in fear. She'd had enough cringing and hiding and hoping against the worst that would inevitably come. She wanted to hope for something better. Milk her children could swallow without gagging. Voice rising: she was thirty-seven years old . . . !

When we finally emerged from the basement it was like blinking at a miracle. In my father's arms, ascending the stairs slowly, squinting into the light with every footfall. I remember stepping into our flat with the two men, my father and our tenant violinist. The windows splayed open. Before leaving they had released the latches on the windows to minimize the impact of the explosions. My father held me to keep me away from shards of broken glass. Wind gusted through the open windows. It seemed to me that the wind was sweeping in the very sky, there was so much cold light. It brought an emptiness into the unlived rooms. A purity. As if all had been swept clean, sterilized by the light and the blue air. Rooms that had lived something we had been spared or denied a life of their own. The men's voices boomed. The flat felt so empty. There were our things, the horsehair recamier and sturdy credenza, the framed photographs, and fringed lampshades, and even the throw rugs Apu stepped over as he hurried eagerly down the hall, checking over everything. But they seemed insubstantial, almost transparent in that windy light. They had lost their solidity. Everything was light and airy as though even the thick oak table could be swept away in a breath of wind. The men's shoes resounded on the hardwood that skirted the carpets. It was as if we had never lived there. As though in our absence someone had cleared out our personal claim to these belongings, leaving frames, merely, that had filled with light. The outline of a sofa, the shadow of an armchair. All had filled with a light that was blue, clear, and so jagged it might slice you if you dared move. I was taken aback when my father laughed and our violinist put his head outside and waved. Human gestures that were incongruous to me, and risky in that rare ether.

We were in a little car, my sister, my father, and me, and we were hurtling past windbreaks on a highway. We were moving so fast, it was strange and wild to me as would be the ride in a Canadian amusement park many years later. Blasting around and around so fast, your teeth ground together, and you couldn't think past the sensation of being propelled without will. That's how I felt sandwiched between my sister and my father, conveyed into the countryside away from everything familiar. My mother's food packets tucked inside his pockets. My mother in her apron on the street, waving goodbye.

Apu had told us many stories of his life before the war on his family's country estate. Even as a baby I knew about the tobacco plantation and horse-drawn carriage. I had heard about crop rotation and imagined the fields spinning like the arms of the windmill in one of my picture books – one year up, one year down. We had grown to imagine all that was good and beautiful to have risen out of his family's turf. The metre-long braided loaves of chalah from my grandmother's kitchen, and the tables set for twelve, sometimes twenty. The people had grown as rich and bountiful as the fields that fed and clothed them. The land they had lived on and nurtured as lovingly as their offspring for three generations. I no more remember hearing these stories for the first time than I do taking my first step. They were part of the climate my sister and I lived in, and we had absorbed them into our psyches – psyche as in soul, ethos, grasp of life. As the seasons bloomed and faded, so had my father's rural past.

Whizzing in a little car, away from my mother and from Budapest, we were going to the country. My father was taking us into the country. Being children, we didn't know what to expect, but we must have expected a great deal.

Spring, ushered by the stench of wet winter rot, assailed us on arrival. And the ground mushy under our feet as though it would suck us in. The sodden fetid air we could only marvel at when our father said with relish, "Smell it? That is the earth blowing out its winter breath." Our offended urban nostrils flared in distaste. Feeling chilly in the damp air, we tramped along the muddy furrows. I looked to my sister for some cue, something to help me interpret the unpleasant sensations made more confusing by my father's obviously happy stride. Her boots seemed to sink into the furrows. Each step, as she pulled it up stickily, was laborious. She was ahead of me by six years. She was my measure, my yardstick. Hers the first impression.

"There was a calf born just this week," my father told us. "Isn't that lucky?" His voice full with the pleasure of giving. But we weren't prepared for the stench in the barn and the rows of enormous beasts with their hot vaporous breaths. He went down the row, patting their sides, pulling up their eyelids. I was like a puppy beneath his feet. I wouldn't take a step away from him. I clung to his trousers until he was forced to pick me up. When he did, when I was up, oh, it was too late to look away. Something you wanted to hide from, but riveting. One by one he had pried their eyes open, but he wasn't expecting disease. Not anything as red, as rawly red as this, in every possible shade of red and plum unfolding like the layered petals of giant bloom all blood and flesh and tissue. A festering bovine backside from whose center a black vermin seeped and crawled. My father sucked back his breath in disbelief, and turned quickly to divert my gaze. But my sister was already retching, a loud, raspy choke and surge.

She doesn't remember this, she claims. And all memory of a newborn calf we might have seen, or baby chicks, or new lambs has been expunged from my collection. But I retain the red gore disease mirrored in my poor father's dismay. He who had grown from the earth, who loved the smell of horse shit and fodder. He could grow a forest in a bed of salt, and in our Ville d'Anjou garden he did grow a veritable arbour of fruit trees and flowering shrubs and beds that never wilted. To see his children repelled so virulently by the living earth, to see us severed from generations who had cultivated this land, people who had loved it and nourished it and built a dynasty from it. How it must have brought home to him all he had lost. Even as he held us in his arms and wiped my sister's streaming nose with his monogrammed handker-

chief. As he stroked our soft hair and cradled our delicate
bones, I could feel him remembering and holding along with
us the other small daughter – the first one, our half-sister –
lost in an Auschwitz oven. He remembered her in each caress
he gave us; in each kiss on our foreheads and flip of a
storybook page, she was beside us, loved just the same. As he
held what was dear to him, how he must have felt the
widening of the chasm that had split his life.

My family left Hungary in 1957. The memory has become a
family icon. My mother's hands locked into each child's. Her
head has turned and is looking over her shoulder at our
father. "With or without you," she is saying as she leads us
down the front walk of the apartment tenement, "we're
going." My father stands indecisively at the building's entrance. He is a man of European height, small only by North
American proportions. His arms hang by his sides, and his
face is carved in loss over loss. As he watches us his face
begins to break down along these creases until it is the face
of our century, its features skewed and misaligned. When he
leaves the portal of that building his figure diminishes with
each step. By the time he reaches us his shoulders are round,
his chest has sunk into his belly. He is the father I now
recognize and the one I really knew. The man who never
again trudged through fields of corn or patted the flanks of
horses, who from that moment was always close by our sides,
our Daddy. A man for whom borders opened, but whose
world shrank around the members of his family.

LÁSZLÓ KEMENES GÉFIN

The Importance of Becoming a Boy Scout

All right, listen, it went like this: Imre Varga took out the bottle of cognac from the brown paper bag, unscrewed the cap, drank, screwed back the cap, and replaced the bottle in the bag. Then he said:

"Actually, if you want to know, it all boils down to one thing: ass."

Now I'm not a hundred percent sure whether he said "ass" or used another word instead, like "sex" or "women" or something like that but it's funny that this is the word that comes to my mind. It's true, by that time we had drunk quite a bit, especially Imre and McIntyre; boy, they almost polished off a bottle of cognac between the two of them, on top of all the beer we'd put away at Toe Blake's and later at Rymark's. Now I'm not saying we were stoned or anything, we all had steak for lunch which is supposed to soak up a lot of booze, or so they say. Imre said that back home before a night of serious drinking he'd go and eat a few heads of onions and drink a pint of cooking oil to lay the proper foundation. Brrrrr, Jesus, what a stomach . . .

Anyway, to get back to Varga and his story. As I said, we were sitting on a bench in Dominion Square, with that bottle of Hennessy in a paper bag under the bench. Every few minutes or so one of us would reach for the damn bottle, take a quick look around and then have a drink. Then the other guy would do the same thing a little bit later. It was unbelievable. I mean, can you picture McIntyre and me, sitting in Dominion Square, on a Saturday afternoon in the merry month of May, drinking secretly from a bottle in a paper bag? Can you? Of course the whole crazy business was

Varga's idea; he said this is how they used to celebrate the
arrival of summer and the reappearance of light summer
dresses on the girls of Budapest. They would sit on a bench
in one of the squares, three or four of them and drink
straight from the bottle which of course, he said, didn't have
to be in a paper bag. The thing was to give a compliment to
every girl that passed by their bench. This was in their
university days or something.

I don't have to tell you that this last part of the ceremony
was omitted by us, I mean McIntyre and me. The thing with
the bottle was crazy enough. But Varga, boy, he was hellbent
on holding up tradition, you know, he started calling to the
girls walking by. He soon gave it up, though, I suppose
because of the looks he got from the girls, they must've
thought he was nuts, but also I guess because McIntyre told
him that if he didn't shut his fucking mouth he'd break the
ceremonial bottle on his fucking head. He said we're not in
Budapest; that the girls of Montreal are not used to this kind
of horseshit, summer dresses or no summer dresses; that he
simply wanted to sit around in the sunshine and get quietly
stewed; that he wanted no trouble with the cops on account
of some goddemn crazy Hungarian acting out his goddemn
nostalgia. "In my present state of mind," he said, "I'm quite
content to just look at the girls, and I advise you to do the
same, if you know what's good for you."

Then shortly after that came the remark about the whole
thing coming down to ass. Yes, it was ass, because I remember what McIntyre said right after that.

"Ass, my ass," he said to Imre Varga. "Jesus, there are
other things beside ass, you know. Christ, it really makes me
so mad to hear you stupid romantic European sons of bitches
whining constantly that you're not getting enough of it as if
there were nothing else of importance to talk about. All
right, OK, granted, it's part of life and all that, but JEEEEE-

SUS, you ought to be old enough to face facts, for heaven's sake. And the facts are as follows. Number one, that sex is bullshit. Number two, that love is for babies. And number three, that women are a necessary nuisance." He sighed and reached for the bottle. "Jesus H. Christ," he added, "these red-hot lovers from Europe, they drive me crazy." He drank and replaced the bottle in the bag. "And another thing," he said, changing the tune. "Most of you whining bastards are usually married to some good looking chick who thinks you're god come down to earth. I know this is the truth in your case. Instead of getting down on your goddemn knees to thank your lucky stars, you go around complaining and shedding tears over the fact that you weren't born an Arab sheik with four wives and fifty concubines. Christ almighty, face up to reality and stop this goddemn whining."

And so on and so forth. You know McIntyre, once he gets going there's no telling where he's going to stop. Especially with a little snaps under his belt . . . Shneps, is it? Well, booze, then, no matter how you care to name it.

Anyway, to get back. Imre Varga wasn't put off by McIntyre's lecture. He just leaned back against the bench, with a profoundly tragic look on his face, you know, melancholy, and all that jazz. But I knew he wouldn't leave things hanging in the air like that. I don't know if I told you but ever since Varga came to work with us, he and McIntyre always found something to argue about. The insults, the taunting, the endless bickering that went on between them was something else. I got a kick out of the whole thing, you know, I wasn't sure whether they were friends or enemies. I usually intervened when they completely exhausted each other, and just sat facing one another, growling insults across the table. "You're a smart ass," McIntyre would say, "and a goddemn dee-pee and a phony and why the fuck don't you go back where you came from." Varga would quietly reply: "You're a barbarian. Why don't you go back where you really belong, among those moronic Highland cave dwellers with no underpants." McIntyre would clench his fists and would jump up, and that's when I made my little entrance, and since they were usually pretty stoned by then, it wasn't too long before I could steer the conversation on to something else. If you call that conversation.

All right, OK, here we go again. So as soon as McIntyre had finished saying his piece, Varga was ready with his own stuff. He spoke in a subdued kind of voice, grave-like, you know. I wasn't sure whether it was for real or if he was acting. This is how it went.

"I can't really expect you to understand me," Imre Varga began. "I'm different from you guys: my background, my experiences, my very genes are different! No, wait, I'll be really and truly honest with you as I've never been before. I mean it. Listen, for God's sake." During his talk Varga constantly had to fence off McIntyre's interruptions. "Look," he continued. "How can I explain to you my feelings about women? To me it is a never-ending battle and a great mystery. I'll give you an example. When I read that Erroll Flynn had over two thousand love affairs during his life, I wasn't myself for days, I was in such lethargy." ("Poor baby," said McIntyre.) "Yes," said Varga, "or when I read the memoirs of Casanova or when I think seriously about people like this Hugh Hefner, I get so depressed that all life loses its flavour for me. You see, this is what you don't seem to understand, either of you. You say that if you screwed one, you screwed them all, and you say that if you were lucky enough to find one who's reasonably decent, then hurray, get down on your knees and thank the Lord." ("Goddamn right," said McIntyre.) "And I say," Varga went on, "that to me woman is like outer space to man, or like what the earth was to the explorers. I can't say that: Well, I'll stop here because the rest of the territory is the same anyhow. No, that's not the way I feel, that's not the way the explorers felt

about the new possibilities, the mysteries, the new con-
quests." ("Poor little Christopher Columbus of Cunt," said
McIntyre. But Varga wasn't disturbed.) For me, it is an
endless process of discovery; the more you discover, the
more you know." He stopped and looked at me. Then he
continued: "I know this may sound like a lot of meaningless
rationalization to you, but I can't help it, I can't help myself,
that's how I am made . . . Women have been the curse and
ruin of my life."

McIntyre went in search of the bottle and took a big
swig. Then he spoke, his voice laced with tremors of hysteria.

"George," he said to me, "I, Robert Douglas McIntyre,
want to make a formal deposition. I wish to state that during
my life I've been subjected to ill-considered and prejudiced,
not to say idiotic babblings of various individuals. But now I
wish to further state that garbage we've been forced to listen
to just now is the most contemptible piece of crap I've ever
encountered. Please tell this gentleman to fuck off."

After a short pause, I said "Fuck off" to no one in
particular.

They are missing the whole thing, I thought. Here is this
really marvellous afternoon, all hazy and golden and everything, and they're missing it all by getting mixed up in useless
hairsplitting talk. They aren't even watching the girls, for
crying out loud. I knew that my time to interrupt hadn't yet
arrived, they weren't as yet grabbing each other by the
throat, but I felt the occasion did warrant extraordinary
measures.

"Look over there," I said to them. "No, no, over there!"
And I pointed to two girls in white tennis outfits sauntering
lazily across the square, carrying rackets and things. I don't
know, was it the booze, Varga's crazy talk of their summer
ceremony, or something else, I don't know, but I felt as if I

was under some kind of spell. Those two girls seemed like the dream of every man: they were tall, graceful and sort of glided by like . . . like swans or something. I'm no poet but I was hit by their beauty, you know, they were very beautiful, but something else, too, they were so . . . so haughty and . . . and vulnerable, I don't know, like some rare birds in a forest. Yes, that's the word, they looked so rare and precious, so . . . so fine . . . I don't know. Of course, I didn't say any of these things to the guys, you know what McIntyre would have said. I only said to Varga: "Come on fella, say hello to those two, and if they want to pick you up, tell 'em you've got a friend who also wants to be an explorer."

But Imre Varga didn't seem to hear me; he hardly paid any attention to the girls who slowly disappeared in the crowd on St. Catherine Street. He only kept looking at McIntyre and he finally spoke.

"Look, I'd like to tell you a little story. The only thing I ask is that it should go no further. I mean, it's not that important but it's personal. The thing is," and you know, Varga tried to appear real serious, solemn and mournful all the time, and I'm still not sure whether it was put-on or he was really in earnest. "The thing is," he said, "all my life I tried to fight my feelings for women. My lust, if you want to call it that. While I was a student I even tried to shut myself off completely, to exclude women entirely from my life. I didn't even look at them. I just kept to my room for months on end and studied. My friends thought I'd gone crazy. But I really wanted to test myself and I wanted to get rid of this constant craving, this yearning for women. The months went by and I grew more and more calm; I truly felt I had conquered temptation or the risk of yielding to temptation. I felt I was reborn. To test this new sense of freedom, I had to go out into the street, among people, to actually be with women. I went to our favourite square and sat down on my bench I hadn't seen for three-four months. For the first time

I allowed myself to look at the girls. I experienced a mounting feeling of joy and triumph: The girls come and go, and I keep looking at them and admiring them but that's all. They didn't do a thing to me. I was free, finally I was free from them. Then, just as I was about to leave, full to the brim with exultation, a small, dark, insignificant-looking girl sat down on the bench beside me. She was nothing special, a plain girl with a book on her knees. So I got up to go and as I passed the girl, her smell, the smell of her body hit me. It was indescribable. It was such a sweet, mysterious, over-powering fragrance that my eyes filled up with tears. I was lost again. I was lost." Varga shook his head. He reached for the bottle again.

McIntyre got really riled up. "Jeeeesus," he said, "this is so typical of you, you know. You want to prove to us what a great hero you are, and all you can prove is that you've got no nuts, no spine, no balls. You've got nothing."

"Maybe too much balls," said Varga with a sad smile. Which made McIntyre even more mad. At that point, I don't know why, I began to feel kind of sorry for Imre Varga. Well, not really sorry, but kind of, I don't know, sympathetic. I said to him, ignoring McIntyre completely:

"All right, for Christ's sake, I believe you." ("I didn't know you were a sucker for this kind of shit," said McIntyre.) "But I just thought of something. Did it ever occur to you that perhaps in your childhood there was something, I don't know, something that happened that made you like this. I mean, I don't know, it's just a thought."

McIntyre acted astonished. "When did you take up amateur psychology, my friend?" he said. But Varga didn't hear him. He just looked at me with great surprise.

"But how did you guess? How did you know? This is exactly what I want to tell you about, how the sickness started, back in the past, almost twenty years ago. You see," he turned to McIntyre, "I need no psychologist to unravel the causes of my problem. I know everything. I am a victim of circumstances; I was born in an unsettled age – that's all. There is no mystery, no unsolved childhood hang-ups, etcetera. I am convinced, you see, that if I had received a more religious upbringing, and if I could've become a boy scout, my whole life would've taken a different turn." He stopped and looked from right to left to measure our reaction.

I don't have to tell you how McIntyre reacted, but even I was kind of disappointed. I thought he really meant to be serious, and now, what kind of new crap was this? But Varga was adamant.

"Please," he said, "let me continue. I am deadly serious. Wait till the end and then judge, not before. Look. First of all, I would like to clear up something. The institution of boy scouts the way we had it back then had no resemblance to what you people have here in North America. In my country it was something entirely different: to belong was the dream of every boy; it was an honour, it was something high and magnificent, like a vocation, or something like that. Anyway, that's the way I felt. Back in 1948 the communists abolished the cub scouts, you know, to prevent boys of my generation ever joining the movement. I was ten years old then, just ready and aching to get into the scouts, and then bang, they shut the gates of paradise before me. Guys who were already in the scouts could stay for a while, but no newcomers were allowed in after that date.

"You have no idea how I felt," continued Varga. "I actually did get sick over it, some fever or other. But while I was in bed I got to thinking, and as soon as I recovered, I began to put my plan into operation. I was going to become a boy scout, if only for myself." ("A closet boy scout! Would you believe it?" interrupted McIntyre.) Varga went on: "And that's what I did. Not only did I conduct myself in my daily life according to the Scout Guide, but I began to collect pieces of uniform and scout regalia. I dug up old issues of "The Hungarian Boy Scout," a pre-war publication. I dressed in my partly home-made scout uniform and read those old dog-eared magazines far into the night, dreaming of jamborees, camping adventures and heroic deeds befitting a real boy scout. I was so dedicated that it was frightening. I was waiting for an occasion when I could demonstrate to the world what a real scout I was. That occasion arrived the following summer, the summer of 1949. And what a summer it was!" ("Please," said McIntyre, "easy on the go, OK?")

"We lived in a large country town," Imre Varga continued, and he named the place but I forget. He said: "But the summer holidays I always spent at my grandparents' who lived in a small village about eighty kilometers from Budapest. These summers stand out in my memory as the happiest days of my life. My grandparents loved and pampered me and spoiled me outrageously; I loved them and respected them in return. I didn't know then that the summer of 1949 would be the last I'd spend with my grandparents; they both died the following winter."

"That summer I arrived at my grandparents' house as a full-fledged cub scout. Just before the trip I had traded the better part of my precious stamp collection for a Lion Cub insignia and a fourth rank merit badge, and with the rest of my paraphernalia all scrubbed and shiny I truly did look like a genuine boy scout. My grandparents were of course simply overawed, not only by my uniform, but also by my seriousness and professional, scout-like conduct. I was courteous, attentive, and ready to help with the sweeping of the yard, working in the garden, getting the milk, and all kinds of other chores. Everyone was impressed by my uniform, especially the boys and girls in my age group who simply stopped and stared at me and my boy scout stuff as if I were a Martian. Most of them had never seen a boy scout before;

so you can imagine what that did to my ego." ("I can well imagine," said McIntyre glumly. He must have been disappointed that there was nothing in Varga's story that he could attack or revile. He looked pretty unhappy and a bit stoned.)

"All right," said Varga, "so within a week of my arrival I was the undisputed leader of the village boys. The small number of boys who remained hostile to me were routed in one campaign. I promptly organized my followers in a tightly-knit scout troop, divided it into two patrols, and I trained them rigidly according to the rules and instructions found in my boy scout magazines. It was really fantastic. We thought, spoke, and acted like so many miniature Knights of the Round Table; I remember it, I remember everything," (here Varga's voice shook a little). "I remember," he went on, "how my boys, most of them near-illiterates and poor as beggars, sat in speechless rapture one moonlit night as I recounted to them the story of Parsifal. They all knew the Scout Law by heart. We thought we were real boy scouts." Varga stopped and wiped his eyes.

For want of anything better to say, McIntyre said, "Let's have a drink." He took out the bottle from the paper bag and raised it to his mouth. He kept it there for a second or two, then he sucked on it a couple of times. "There's no more left," he said. He got up a little unsteadily and dropped the bag in a nearby waste basket. He returned to the bench with a great sigh, and Varga continued his story.

"I also fell in love that summer for the first time in my life," he said. "Now comes the goofy stuff," said McIntyre and involuntarily rubbed his hands together. That bastard won't shut up, I said to myself. One more peep out of him and he'll get it. Varga went on with the story.

"There was a little girl next door who obviously fell in love with me the day I arrived." ("Obviously," said McIntyre happily. I let that one go by.) "She was, I remember, not very pretty; she was just a strong, sun-tanned little peasant girl with long braided blond hair; mostly I remember her enormous eyes and her strong brown arms. She kept following me everywhere; in fact, I had to make her honorary cub scout. When occasionally we were left alone, she always sidled closer and closer to me and wanted to kiss. Imagine what a spot I was in! I found all her foolishness and this business of kissing totally incompatible with boy scout ethics; and I, her superior, ordered her to stop her unscoutlike behaviour. At the same time, especially on seeing her sad face, something told me that it was certainly against the Boy Scout Oath to hurt someone else's feelings. So I had to compromise, and I allowed her to kiss me once a day when we had to go to get the milk at night at the other end of the village and I let her hold my hand in the cool darkness of the church during evening vespers." ("Two-faced son of a bitch even then," said McIntyre. Behind Varga's back I gave McIntyre a rather vicious stab around the kidneys which made him shut up for a while.) "The little girl's name was Marika," said Varga. "She was my slave.

"But it wasn't Marika I fell in love with, not at first anyway. About ten days after I arrived, a cousin of hers came to spend a week or two with Marika's family. She was from Budapest and her name was Anna. Anna Gál." (I think that was the name.) "She was everything that Marika wasn't. She was white and fragile like a flower. I was particularly fascinated by her lips which were, in contrast to her white skin, thick and dark red; and by her hair which fell back and heavy on her thin shoulders and down her back. Of course I didn't know what was happening to me; I only knew that whenever I saw her, even from a distance, I was seized by a nameless terror. At the same time I wanted to worship her, to be her protector, to throw myself at her feet.

"Since I was the central attraction of the village kids, I took it as a great insult that Anna hardly even noticed me; or at least that was the impression she gave. She spoke to no one except her cousin Marika; and Marika was apparently equally fascinated by her sophistication and big city airs, because she began to spend more and more time with Anna, whispering, giggling, gesticulating. No doubt she must have also noticed how I stood and gaped every time I was near Anna. I'm sure she made every effort in her little power to keep me from meeting Anna.

"But a meeting was unavoidable, although I myself dreaded it the most. One afternoon I was picking mulberry leaves for my grandfather's silk worms when I saw Anna approach the tree on which I was working. I didn't know what to do: climb further up and hide among the branches, or come down? I thought of hiding at first, but then I froze. What if she's already seen me and knows I'm up the tree? That would be the end of me. So, trying to hide my horrible nervousness, I climbed down the tree to face her.

"'Are you really a boy scout, Imre Varga?' That was the first thing she said to me," said Varga, shaking his head with a trace of a smile. "I stammered something, a kind of 'yes', and looked at her for an instant. She was even more beautiful from close up, but somehow in my terror I noticed that her right eye was bigger than her left. I tried to dismiss this idiotic notion, and tried to listen to her talk, for she went on speaking to me, disregarding my dumbness and silence. I remember she spoke of her brother who was sixteen and a Scout Leader in Budapest, and that he was expected to arrive in our village in a few days time. She left soon after that, and I gathered the mulberry leaves that got scattered all over under the tree when I climbed down in my panic. I walked home in a daze, in a strange euphoria. She spoke to me, I said to myself over and over, she actually spoke to me.

"For a few days I could only get a glimpse, here and there, of Anna. We didn't speak again. Even though I knew

I loved her . . . Yes, loved her," said Varga emphatically, "I loved her, I was only eleven, but I know I had it, I had the feeling, if you've never felt it, it's no use." Varga waved wearily as he continued. "Anyway, even though I loved her, I just couldn't work up enough courage to walk over to her house – she lived next door! – and ask her to go for a walk or a swim or something. Instead, I tried to concentrate on some military exercises with my troops, but became less and less enthusiastic about the whole thing. I remember sending the boys home, telling them I wasn't feeling well. I then went to my secret hiding place behind the barn, and dreamed of Anna.

"The following Sunday afternoon Marika came over and asked me if I wanted to go to the movies. I was surprised that she came to see me at all, after the way she had behaved since Anna appeared on the scene. I wanted to go to the movies anyway, but now that she asked me I had to feign indifference and finally I said I'm not sure. Then suddenly Anna came to my mind. Yes, perhaps she'll be there, too. Maybe I can sit somewhere near her or just know that she's there. So I proceeded to change my mind and announced to Marika that I'd go with her. I didn't dare ask, of course, whether Anna will be coming or not; and Marika didn't volunteer that information.

"I put on my full Lion Cub uniform, badges and all, and went with Marika to the movie house in the centre of the village. I remember noticing how obediently and humbly Marika walked beside me, as if to atone for her previous behaviour. She was dressed in her usual Sunday dress, a little blue thing, but I noticed that she was wearing a pair of new yellow sandals, most likely a present from Anna's parents who were supposed to be 'rich.' I furtively glanced at her from time to time as she walked beside me. Somehow I had the feeling that she was different, maybe prettier, I don't know.

"There was the usual big crowd at the theatre waiting for tickets. In vain did I search all over for Anna. I kept looking around right up to the minute we had to go inside and take our seats. But she didn't come. I felt like going home, but of course I couldn't leave Marika, it was unthinkable." Imre Varga again smiled and shook his head. McIntyre sat with a bland face, as if he weren't even listening. Varga resumed his talk.

"We went in. No sooner did the movie begin when I felt Marika's fingers squeeze my hand. She squeezed hard, then soft, then she stroked my palm with trembling fingers, then she squeezed again. We remained motionless for a long time; then she continued to play with my hand. Then, just as I was about to withdraw from this game of hers, she reached over with her hand and put it on my arm. I felt her leaning closer and closer against my shoulder, and I heard her whisper: 'I love you, Imre, I love you.' Her lips brushed against my lips as she whispered those words, and suddenly, I don't know from where, I felt a great wave of heat flash through my whole being. It was scary and at the same time so thrilling, so new, so delicious. I don't know what made me do it: I squeezed Marika's hand back, in fact I squeezed it so hard I heard her gasp. But I felt her bend down and then felt her kissing my hand, and slowly she began to pull it, my hand toward her, closer and closer. Finally, she placed my hand on her thigh. She let go of my hand and then just pressed it to her bare skin, gently but firm . . . "

Here McIntyre couldn't stand it any more. "Oh my beloved sweet Lord Jesus Christ," he groaned as if someone had stabbed him in the chest. "How long, oh Lord, how long? Why dost thou inflict upon Thy faithful servant such cruel and unjust punishment? Have I not been . . ."

I cut him off. "Oh go on and bugger yourself," I said to

him. "Can't you keep quiet, for God's sake? Why can't you shut your trap and just listen to this nice story?"

"Do you hear that, Varga?" McIntyre sneered. "He called your syrupy crap a nice story. You should be pleased, you have just made a new convert to your kind of sentimental European garbage. And you," he turned to me, "don't you have enough sense to see through all that junk? Don't you see he is inventing the whole thing right here in front of us?"

"JESUS!" I yelled. "LET HIM FINISH HIS GODDAMN STORY! If you're not interested, why the hell don't you get your fat ass out of here? Huh? Why sit through it all if it's such an agony for you? And I know why, too. Because you're just as . . . "

He didn't let me finish. "Shut your trap, you goddamn birdbrain," he said and glared at me menacingly. But I felt his voice lacked its usual conviction, or something like that. He crossed his legs and turned his back to us. "Go on," I said to Varga. "What happened next?"

Varga didn't seem to pay attention to us. He was lost in thought. He looked at me, kind of slow, and thoughtful, and than automatically reached under the bench for the bottle which wasn't there any more. He straightened up, and turned a little toward me. Then he continued.

"You must know," he said, "that there was complete darkness in the theatre. There was no emergency lighting or things like that. It was pitch dark, nobody could see a thing. With my palm pressed to Marika's thigh the whole world vanished for me, the entire universe ceased to exist. There was nothing but this heat, this fire inside me, and the feel of Marika's smooth skin. I didn't know what was happening to me; but as if having a power of their own, my fingers began to explore her flesh. Then suddenly I was seized by a terrible rush of fear and anxiety. What are you doing? – a voice said to me. What kind of boy scout are you? I trembled all over. I suddenly remembered the last command of the Boy Scout Oath, that I will do my best to keep myself physically strong, mentally awake, and morally straight. How can I describe it? As if there were two armies fighting a battle inside me. Because all that time my hand was on Marika's bare thigh, and the strange fire just wouldn't go out. The voice I heard slowly receded, and I heard another voice, the voice of the fire saying, you're not really a boy scout. You're not a boy scout at all, so never mind the oath. And then again I felt her hand on mine, pressing it down on her thigh. And I was lost. My fingers continued to grope further and further up, until they could go no further. My hand became paralyzed and I didn't dare do anything; I just held it there for a few seconds which seemed like eternity. ("Oh Jesus, oh God," said McIntyre faintly.) "Then slowly I took my hand away, and neither of us made a move after that. A little later the lights came on for the intermission. Marika got up immediately and rushed out. I didn't have a chance to look at her face. She mumbled something about coming back right away.

"It took me at least three or four minutes to muster enough courage to turn and take a look in the theatre. I turned around and I felt the floor would cave in under me. Sitting directly behind me, about five rows back, there was Anna, proud and beautiful. I remember she wore a snow white dress which sort of radiated in the semi-darkness of the theatre. Beside her sat a tall looking boy in a scout uniform. I turned back as fast as I could, closed my eyes and began praying like I've never prayed before: Please God, please make them not notice me, please, please forgive me, please just this once. But at the same time I still felt Marika's skin on my hand and my face was burning hot.

"I was still lost in fervent prayer when I heard someone sit down beside me in Marika's seat. But I knew it wasn't her. It was the boy scout sitting beside Anna.

"'I'm Péter Gál,' he said to me. His voice sounded friendly but I didn't dare look at him. I felt his eyes examining me all over, my phony uniform, my badges, everything. I felt like crawling into a hole, I felt like apologizing to somebody I don't know what for. I was glued to my seat, numb and terrified, a powerless piece of jelly. ("Now you're talking," said McIntyre, but his voice was flat and far-away-like. Varga didn't hear him. He just went on.) "The scout, seeing I didn't make any answer, spoke again. 'I'm a Life Scout in the Saint-Something Lyceum in Budapest,' he said. Anna told me a lot of things about you, that you're a Lion Cub and that you organized the boys in the village. That was really nice. What troop do you belong to at home?' I opened my mouth to say something but nothing came out, nothing, not a sound. Then he asked: 'What's the name of your patrol?' Again, nothing. I just shook my head like an idiot. I was incapable of uttering a single sound. Then Anna's brother asked me what was my troop number? The same result: deathly silence, or perhaps a tiny squeak from the bottom of my throat.

"Then I heard him laugh," Imre Varga said in a low voice. "It was short and good-natured, a friendly sort of laughter. 'Come on,' he said, 'you don't have to be so nervous, it's all right. Do you like being a scout?' I felt myself nodding affirmatively and then I heard him laugh again. 'That's the main thing,' he said, and he gave me a quick pat on the shoulder.' Good luck to you now. Oh, another thing. Don't tell Anna that I told you but she'd like you to come over more often. She's a bit shy, you know, but I think she really likes you.' He got up to go. 'Be prepared,' he said, and with that went back to his seat.

"The lights dimmed and the second half of the film began. I don't remember anything about the film; I just sat there engulfed in my shame and anguish. A few seconds later I heard Marika sneak back to her seat. She didn't say a word;

she only took my hand. That did it. Slowly, all the pain and
shame began to dissolve in a sort of feeling of gratitude
toward her, toward Marika. Big tears started to roll down
my cheeks and I didn't care whether she noticed them or not.
The tears stopped after a while, and we just continued
holding hands till the end of the movie."

Imre Varga took a deep breath and then continued.

"Epilogue. After that Sunday afternoon Marika and I
became practically inseparable. I spent almost all my time
with her; in fact the following week I formally disbanded my
troop of village scouts. I still went on wearing my uniform
for a while but during the last days of my stay in my
grandparents' village I gave away my badge and scout tie to
one of the kids. Anna? I never saw her again. I vaguely
remember Marika telling me that the following Tuesday or
Wednesday they had to go back to Budapest. But I kept
dreaming about her for months after that, I longed for her
and never forgot her. So that's how it was," Varga said,
wearily. "Maybe I'm still searching for Anna . . . "

"Yes," said McIntyre, rousing himself from his half-
slumber; at least that's how it looked to me. "Yes, and all you
find is Marikas all over the place." He yawned and streched
his arms. "What crap," he said, and got up. "I don't know
about you guys," he said, "but after this heart-rending confession I feel like taking a leak. After that I'll have a beer and
then go home. Enough is enough."

We all got up.

As we were walking towards Rymark's Tavern on the
western side of the square, a bit dizzy and dazed, at least
that's the way I felt, I wanted to say something to Varga,
something comforting.

"Look," I said, "maybe, maybe your thing, whatever it
is, has nothing to do with this boy scout business and Marika

and the other girl. I mean, who knows what really happened, I mean, hell, shit, don't take it like that . . . "

Varga didn't answer right away. He walked on straight and pretty steady, only he was kind of pale. Then he said: "I don't know. All I know is that I should have become a boy scout, that's all. And I swear to you," he said and stopped, looking at his shoes. "I swear that my son whenever he comes of age, my son, he will join the boy scouts. I swear to you." Then he continued walking. I guess he did feel the booze a little after all.

McIntyre was walking ahead but he must've heard what Imre Varga said, and he couldn't let that one pass.

"Atta boy, Varga," he said, turning back, which almost made him lose his balance. "Atta boy, Varga, m'lad! Under your expert guidance your little explorer will turn out to be a regular Galahad in no time. In no time at all."

We entered the tavern and McIntyre shouted to the waiter. "Harry, six drafts on the double!"

We all went to the toilet, and when we came back to our table, the six glasses of foaming beer were already there waiting for us. We sat down and McIntyre said: "Gentlemen, I want to propose a toast." He picked up his glass without spilling a drop. Then he said, "I want to propose a toast to Varga's son here, the future Eagle Scout, the future Knight of the Round Table." He swayed a fraction of an inch and glared at Imre Varga as if expecting a reply. But Imre Varga was silent.

"And while we're at it," McIntyre continued, "how about a toast to . . . to . . . to what's-his-name? What was his name, Varga?" He looked straight in Imre Varga's eye.

"Péter Gál," said Varga quietly.

"That's it, that's the one," said McIntyre, still holding up the glass, still not taking his eyes off Imre Varga. Now that I think of it, it seems his voice shook a little, just for an instant. "A toast to Péter Gál then," he said, "wherever he may be."

We drained our glasses.

That was the end of the afternoon.

Boy, that beer sure tasted good, especially after that hard stuff.

TOM KONYVES

The Tree of Singing Birds

On Dias de las Meurtas
the sacred day of remembrance
bright red long-stemmed flowers appeared
bright orange flowers, yellow
petals, trails of petals
to every corner, church bells ring
as hundreds of birds
converge on the square
in the tree of the square
the tree of singing birds

how it endures the lone violin
and the silent poem of my pen

Postcard

In your poems lovers
are separated, sometimes
by miles, sometimes heartbeats,
modes of living, sharing spaces.
I was in New York when Lennon
was shot, you were in Hawaii,
his killer's home.
So much for coincidence.
The spectre of the tropical sun
has not found its way to Montreal
where record freezing temperatures have numbed,
and hypnotized me, held hostage my *joie de vivre*
until now, when Time assaults me in the parking lot
and I empty my heart's vault, delighting in Change.

Back Alley

Back alley laundry and children,
miniature gardens, incessant drill.
Sunbathers and migrating pigeons,
nervous sparrows.

And it's these sparrows, by God,
who repeat all our thoughts
in their infernal dialogues,
in their gossip not meant for us
watching rainbuckets mirror
the stately Versailles.

Vancouver Rag

The leader of the opposition
is dragged from the House.
A black vulture glides to a stop
at the side of the highway.

Joggers brush past me around Stanley Park,
smiling. I can't figure out,
in a historical sense. The very profile
of the sun washes everything away,
or is it the other way around?
(Don't call him by his first name,
his camera might sprout thorns.)
Subdominant bass lines walk
hand in hand down the aisle of love.
I pose for a picture –
with monogrammed chrome side-view mirror.

Surrounded by oil portraits of dogs,
chinese cabinets, porcelain turkeys,
brass candlesticks, urns demanding
the pastoral trio to work the fading garden,
garbed in silk, subtle silver chain in tow.

Give and take. I separate myself
from my work, walk down to the beach
with mindless desire for the remote mountains
where my words turn to hopeless prayer
and my body to a glowing meteor.

JOHN MARLYN

Good for You, Mrs. Feldesh

When she came to Main Street, the old woman paused and, as in an old familiar ritual, stopped and slowly turned completely around to look at the sign on the roof.

"The Place," it said in rich green and gold. But it was the figure of the man and girl above that held her attention. Just barely outlined in red neon, she could make of them almost what she wished, the man handsome and tenderly whispering, the girl graceful and slender.

Her lips parted as she looked up at them, dancing there against the night sky. Three distinct steps they took together and with every step the man's head drew closer to his partner's; but never would his lips touch hers. At the third step, when she felt he was about to kiss her, both figures vanished.

"Maybe it is better that way," the old woman said to them. "Worse things could happen, believe me."

Her feet ached.

Once more the dancing girl began lowering her head to that shoulder it would never rest upon.

The old woman nodded. Five hours it had taken her to clean and scrub and wax in there. But now everything in the dance hall shone and sparkled. She smiled because she liked to think of it that way.

Her back ached. Only four days ago she had been to see Dr. Mueller, recommended by Mrs. Stengel.

"'Pains in my back and legs,' I told him," she muttered. "And he says, 'Go home – don't worry. There's nothing wrong.'"

Tears came to her eyes. "But with Mrs. Stengel who's as fat as a pig, she comes to him with the same pains and he gives her medicine and says, 'Come back next week.'"

She walked on. The silence of the dark streets reminded her of that deeper night-silence on the farm and her early years in this country. Lying awake in bed night after night, listening, she would hear it, always at the same time, the far-away plaintive cry of the train whistle, giving voice, it seemed to her, to all the lonely men and women lying awake as she was, a stranger in the terrifying immensity of the midnight prairie.

But to think of that farm was to think of the money they had lost because stubbornly and violently her husband Demetrius had insisted on keeping it in Hungarian kronen. Nine days after they arrived in Canada, the first World War had started and it became worthless.

When she tried to get it changed into Canadian money her husband had objected; when she insisted, he had turned really ugly and threatened her, and that was the end of it.

What they had suffered the first winter, she didn't want to remember.

But it would still be there, that money he had clung to, in that old tobacco tin under the pile of stones where he had hidden it in the northeast pasture.

The stones formed a mound a few feet from the fence and the road that led to town, a town not so very much larger than her village in the old country. But when was it that she had so unexpectedly seen for the first time how very different things were here in this new land? Different even beyond what was so visible; the wooden sidewalks, the drugstore, the bank, and a little restaurant owned by a Chinese man – the first Chinese man she had ever seen. She had gone up and down the street in front of his restaurant half a dozen times or more that first Saturday night just to look at him.

In the fourth year after their arrival it must have been, in the year Andreas had all that trouble with his teeth. She had taken him to town and after leaving the dentist, had gone for a short walk. It was good to be away from the farm and in a cool clean dress again. Here and there, strangers, men and women, moving about their lawns and front gardens, nodded to her as she passed by.

She had seen Mr. and Mrs. Collins on their verandah and they must certainly have caught sight of her, so there was no time to turn back. Mrs. Collins was in a rocking chair, her husband sitting on the top step.

Mrs. Collins was reading the newspaper.

Andreas said something and tugged at her hand.

She scarcely heard him. She had never seen or even heard of such a thing – a woman reading a newspaper. She stared in astonishment across at the woman who so calmly went on reading.

It looked silly and unnatural, as though a hen were to get up one morning and start to crow. She felt like laughing.

Mrs. Collins lowered her head. "Tom," she said, "be a dear and give me the second half, will you?"

Tom – Mr. Collins – was the wealthiest man in the town. Whenever she had seen him in the general store which he owned, she had always crept away and never daring to ask him to attend her, had always waited for one of his younger clerks.

And now here – she moistened her lips and thought of those dark villages in the old country, and of what would have happened to a woman who would have dared to make such a spectacle of herself, and still gazing in confusion at the two people sitting there had already started to walk on when Mrs. Collins looked fully at her. Anna lowered her head. Ever since that shameful night in town in the summer of their second year in the country, she had tried to avoid Mrs. Collins.

The streets had been crowded with farmers like themselves, laughing and talking, and it had been exciting after the lonely weeks on the farm to be with people again, to see the lights in the drugstore window and the barber shop and to look once again at the Chinese owner of the restaurant. She had forgotten that all of this, the bright movement of people and their talk which was such a pleasure to her, was a thing which Demetrius dreaded.

She stopped at Collins' store window to look at a dress, and Demetrius, evidently unaware that she was not beside him, walked on a few steps until finding himself alone, returned, and with a backhanded blow sent her reeling off the wooden sidewalk and into the ditch beside the road.

There was water in it; she remembered standing there in a daze, thinking only that she was wearing her best shoes and stockings, when a man stretched down a hand and pulled her back up to the sidewalk. It was not until then that she heard the shouting and saw the men around Demetrius pushing against him. One of them struck him, and then another, and for a moment she wondered what he had done to provoke them.

She saw him standing there as though stupefied by what was happening, then breaking through, he grabbed her hand and was about to run when a policeman appeared. He placed himself in front of them.

Voices from the crowd came to her. She understood little, but sufficiently; this man – Demetrius, they meant – had struck this woman. "But I'm his wife," she wanted to protest and felt the policeman's eyes upon her and saw herself as she must have appeared to him, her hair coming undone, her shoes and stockings and the hem of her dress covered with mud.

"My husband ain't –" she stammered. "He didn't mean –" and found no words to finish what she wanted to say and began to cry, not only because of the disgrace that had come upon them, but it was not the first time that they had been in trouble with an official in this country. The policeman might already know that they were the same people who had police trouble before because this was the man who had beaten one of his harvest labourers.

She gazed across at the policeman as contritely as she could. We – we are sad," she said, but the policeman was looking at Demetrius.

"No beat wife anymore," the policeman said slowly and distinctly, and to emphasize what he was saying raised his hand and with his forefinger prodded Demetrius on the chest. "You understand?" he said. "No beat wife or you get in trouble."

And that was all. They were free to go. She tugged at Demetrius' arm.

In all her married life, she had never seen him so afraid. He had already learned that it was not permitted to strike others. But he hadn't known that he could not strike his wife. And seeing him there in such fear, trying so painfully to understand, she suddenly felt sorry for him.

The people around them began to move on. As she turned with Demetrius, she saw Mrs. Collins standing behind the window of the store.

She was a buxom elderly woman who on Saturday nights helped in the store, quietly, leisurely waiting on her friends and acquaintances. There was a dignity about her that attracted Anna, and a feeling that she could only describe by saying that Mrs. Collins seemed to respect herself. How long it seemed to her she had been hoping that one night in the store Mrs. Collins would smile at her and walk over and ask her if she could be of help.

Looking at her on that night, as she looked at her now, she wondered how much Mrs. Collins had seen.

But Mrs. Collins swung forward in her rocking chair and smiled.

"Hello, Mrs. Feldesh," she said. "Going for a walk?"

Mr. Collins raised his head and smiled too. "Been a hot day, hasn't it?" he said.

But how could this be, she wondered. The richest people in town. How could they be so friendly to her? She didn't know what to say, and shyly nodded and finally said "yes" and walked quickly away.

For months afterwards, she remembered that afternoon. Then it grew dim.

There was work to do. She helped in the fields sometimes. And she had her own kitchen garden to tend and there were the children and the house and the chickens to look after.

She bought her first piece of store soap and Demetrius threw it out of the window. One day a man in a covered wagon came to the farm; he was a baker and he would come every day if she wanted. She bought a loaf and Demetrius squashed it into a lump and threw it at her. She bought a little box of face powder to use on the Saturdays she went to town and Demetrius never noticed, but she didn't use it on Sundays when they went to church because it seemed wicked.

The old woman glanced over her shoulder at a store she had passed and slowly made her way back to stand and stare with eyes brightening and the stern lines of her mouth softening into a smile at the figure of a little girl in the window, in immaculate white shoes and stockings, in a crisp pink little dress.

Still nodding, she sighed and smiling again, walked on.

She began thinking of that day on which that woman had appeared, a middle-aged woman, on a Monday morning when she was doing the washing.

She announced that she was Miss MacKinnon, the new district nurse, and that she was glad of this opportunity to introduce herself.

To introduce? What did that mean?

Ashamed of her appearance and the disorder in the kitchen, dreading that they had once again violated some law or custom in this country, she nevertheless managed to smile at her as she led her to the front room – the parlor, she remembered it was called in English.

"Will you come to the parlor," she asked, and pleased with herself, continued, "I will go and – and come right away back."

In the bedroom she slipped into a fresh dress and removing her kerchief, arranged her hair.

A district nurse. She considered this. It sounded as though she were a state official. But how? Could a woman be an official in this country?

She returned to her visitor in the front room. She had scrubbed the floor here and polished the furniture only on Saturday. The blinds were half down. It was cool. Everything was clean and tidy.

The woman's first words frightened her. She had come because of Albert.

What could he have done? "He's sick!" she cried.

The woman shook her head. "We think Albert needs glasses," she said calmly. "Reading glasses," she explained, and raising both hands to her eyes blinked through the circles she made with her fingers.

"Aaah, eyeglasses," Anna exclaimed triumphantly.

They laughed together and unexpectedly she liked the woman, even if she was dressed a little too much like a man.

She was thin and dark and no longer young, but there was something fresh about her in that neat-fitting suit and the small white collar on her blouse.

They looked at one another. If only she could understand better, Anna thought, and listened. If only she would stay, if only for a little while longer, to break the silence of the lonely weeks and months so that she could talk, just talk to another woman, to someone who understood.

"Will you maybe." She flushed. What were the words? "Coffee to have?" she said desperately, "and cake – a little cake. Please to say yes?"

Was she mistaken? It seemed to her that the nurse – what was her name? – while moving in her chair, glanced quickly once more around her.

"For once the washing can wait." Anna ran out excitedly; added wood to the fire to keep the washtub water heating; the kettle was still boiling.

Half an hour later they were still talking, and she was aware of the time passing and proud that this fine, educated woman should find sufficient pleasure in her company to stay so long. She said something that Anna failed to grasp. But then clearly she heard, as Miss MacKinnon pursed her lips: "I do all I can to help those people, Mrs. Feldesh, but they're not so poor they can't afford a bar of soap and a scrubbing brush. My superior says I'm too hard on them, but I'm not. I know what it is to be poor. When my family settled here my father had only the strength of his arms and his will – the will to make something of himself. We lived practically on oatmeal, Mrs. Feldesh."

Anna nodded and groped to say that one of the things she liked in this country was that people were not afraid to admit they had once been poor.

Miss MacKinnon nodded too and in a moment of unexpected silence Anna asked her, because it was the first thing that came to her mind and because it was easy to express, how one prepared this oatmeal.

But an oatmeal pudding and cookies and with a prune filling. She shuddered.

". . . Cheap, nourishing and wholesome food, Mrs. Feldesh. I'm delighted you asked me," the nurse concluded and glanced at her watch. "But now I must go."

Anna walked with her to the gate where Miss MacKinnon's horse and little buggy stood. They remained for a moment absently watching the farmer in the next field working at a stump.

"He's certainly working hard," Miss MacKinnon said.

"Yes," Anna replied. "He's a real bugger –" and sensed instantly from the woman's expression that what she had said was wrong, that what she had always feared had now happened.

"It's bad?" she asked and seeing the scarlet flush on the woman's face realized that it must be not merely wrong but indecent.

"A real bugger for punishment," Andreas had exclaimed, seeing the same farmer last winter chopping down a tree.

Sadly she looked across at this woman whom she liked so very much and whom she admired and had so anxiously hoped to make her friend.

"He works strong – hard, I mean," she stammered. "I heard somebody say when he's a hard worker, he's a bugger for punishment."

"It's not a nice word, Mrs. Feldesh."

The nurse thanked her for the coffee and cake, got into her buggy and smiled in a way that still seemed friendly, Anna thought, as she opened the gate.

Miss MacKinnon had already raised the reins and settled back in her seat when she lowered them and looked earnestly down at her.

"Mrs. Feldesh," she said. "People sometimes say I'm a little too forward. They've intimated I'm officious."

Anna stared up at her in wonder.

"I hope you won't mind what I'm going to say, Mrs. Feldesh," the nurse continued. "Believe me when I say it's well meant. If you lived in the city I'm sure you would long ago have found your way to an English class at night school."

"To school?" Anna cried. "Me!" and drew away in sudden fright. "But where to school? Not with my own children?"

Her laughter sounded unnatural to her.

"No, Mrs. Feldesh. At night with Miss Butler, their teacher. Why don't you think about it? If you like, I'll mention it to her."

"No," Anna said. "Please not say anything. I will think about it first, thank you. I enjoyed so much to talk to you."

Miss MacKinnon had raised the reins again. "And I enjoyed it too, Mrs. Feldesh, and thank you again. But now I must really be off."

The old woman paused on the corner of Logan Avenue. She was tired, and she was hungry.

"But where was I," she said, and remembered that through her fears and all her apprehensions there had remained, fixed in her mind, the image of herself on her own porch one evening reading the newspaper, or a book even, and saw herself quietly and easily talking to a delighted Miss MacKinnon and on a Saturday in the store to Mrs. Collins. How surprised they would be.

She smiled and wondered how it would feel to be able to read English and suddenly she wished that nurse had never set foot in her house. How did she know that she had not grown too stupid? And what would happen if she started and failed and everybody heard of it?

The next afternoon, a few minutes after school closed, she crept quietly to the open doorway of the schoolroom and waited. The teacher, a slender woman with brown hair and grey eyes, sat at her desk sorting papers.

"Oh – it's Mrs. Feldesh," she said. "Please come in. Is something the matter, Mrs. Feldesh?" She rose and offered her a chair.

"No – please. Nothing is wrong." Anna moistened her lips.

"Miss Butler." She lowered her hand to the desk to stop from shaking. "I want please you should-make me – do me a big favour."

"Why, I'd be glad to."

Anna shook her head and tried to smile. "Please not say yes yet. You don't know what I'm going to ask. I want you should show me – learn me to read and write."

She felt the heat-flush on her cheeks rising to her forehead as she watched intently the sign of a smile, or even of laughter, for anything that would tell her what the woman was thinking.

In fact, Miss Butler was smiling, "I'd be happy to, Mrs. Feldesh."

Anna lowered her head. "You're a good – you're good," she mumbled.

Miss Butler shook her head. "I'm a teacher, Mrs. Feldesh. I like to teach. Would you like to start this evening?"

"Tonight!" Anna looked at her in alarm. Leaning across the desk, she whispered: "Nobody should know, Miss Butler. It should be a secret. Please to promise me."

"I think we can do that," the teacher said quietly. "Would it be convenient then for you to come to my home? I live with my sister whom we can trust to be silent."

And so it was arranged. But adamantly Miss Butler refused even to hear of being paid. Anna returned home that afternoon with her first lesson to do.

Late that night in the parlor, with Demetrius and the children asleep, she sat at the little table beside the sofa with the first clean page of her exercise book before her.

Again and again as the weeks passed by she went to bed with the frightening conviction that she would never learn.

Sometimes in the silent peaceful hours she would look down at her lesson and remember the longing to be doing what she was doing now. The day was coming very soon when she would be able to open a book or a newspaper and read what was in it.

The summer passed and the winter, and she was no longer afraid to present herself at Miss Butler's door.

Sometimes when her lessons were done, she would open the Eaton's catalogue and it was a joy to read for herself what was written there.

When her secret became known it no longer mattered. Who could laugh at her now when she had already mastered the subjunctive mood? Who would care?

Appropriately, it was Mrs. Collins who first congratulated her. For the first time, too, she had waited on her. Anna was leaving the store when Mrs. Collins drew her behind the rack of cotton dresses, smiled at her and whispered, "Good for you, Mrs. Feldesh. I hope you don't mind my mentioning it. We're all proud of you."

On the wagon on the way home, Anna began to sing to herself until she noticed that Demetrius was glaring at her. She grew silent then.

But why should he, and her sons too, object so violently because she was learning to read and write? The time she spent at Miss Butler's or at her lessons was not time stolen from him or the family. She still looked after them, cooked their meals, and kept them and the house too, clean and neat, and did her work about the farm.

When they got home, Demetrius would probably kick the door open because it was stuck, or yell and roar or perhaps break something.

More he didn't dare to do, at least not out in the open.

Yet the thought persisted that what she was doing was unnatural. Were they right then and she wrong? But then the thought came to her one night that Mrs. Collins would never have asked herself this question and neither would Miss MacKinnon nor Miss Butler. And for the first time it struck here that Mrs. Collins and these other women had a regard for themselves that she lacked.

Perhaps, she reflected, when she had learned to read and write she too would look upon herself in that way. She began to smile.

The old woman looked up and smiled too. Late in summer, almost two years after she had started, the lessons came to an end.

She stood on that night, outside Miss Butler's door, and then on the road looking back, not wanting to go home yet, but to be with people who would somehow make real for her what she had accomplished. She wished she could have spoken with Mrs. Collins, or better still with Miss MacKinnon. It seemed wrong that she should be alone tonight, that this wonderful night should pass as though nothing happened.

She walked on up the hill from the top of which she could see her house. The lamp was on in the kitchen and that was as it should be, but then faintly she heard a sound that

was only too familiar. She became frightened. As she reached
the back door, she heard Demetrius shouting in the kitchen
and Andreas and Jeno encouraging him. There was the crash
of something breaking. She opened the door and saw Felix
at the foot of the stairs and behind him Albert and the girls,
all of them laughing and screaming with pleasure at the sight
of their father who stood drunkenly swaying in his underwear in front of the stove, smashing a chair against it. Her
old exercise books and her readers lay torn and scattered on
the floor. She ran past him, got the younger children upstairs, and came down again as Demetrius tore the last few
pages out of one of her textbooks. She looked past him as
she came into the room, at Andreas and Jeno leaning back
against the table, their eyes coldly, almost indifferently, upon
her.

"I'll kill you –" Demetrius said in English.

He repeated the words and coming toward her, looked
in that expressionless and yet sinister way around him at the
doors and windows, that told her only too clearly what he
was going to do. As his arm rose to strike her, she resolved
for the first time not to accept it, and quaking and forcing
herself to remain erect and not to shield herself, stared back
at him, into those dull, unfeeling eyes she knew so well.

"No," she said. "No," and watched trembling as he
leaned forward to gape at her and turn away one lurching
step and come back again to peer into her face. Then he
turned his head once more away from her and she followed
his gaze to Andreas and Jeno who stood silently watching
and waiting, and with her heart sinking, she understood
what he would now do, what he would have to do to uphold
himself before them.

He raised his hand again slowly and looked at his sons
who unwaveringly looked back at him. And then before she
knew that he had made the decision, he struck her, his first

blow numbing her. She covered her face with her hands as he hit her again, and suddenly she found herself on the floor against the edge of the bottom stair, with a pain so sharp in her back that she began to scream and stopped because it might frighten the children upstairs.

After awhile she crawled upstairs to the bedroom.

The old woman looked up. She remembered every knot-hole in the ceiling above that bed. Her back ached.

An old affliction this, and it had started that night he had beaten her. For weeks afterwards she had been unable to get out of bed and had to get their neighbour's eldest daughter, Bertha, a silent, stolid girl, to come and help with the housework. Nearly a month later she was still dragging herself apathetically through the house. Mrs. Collins sent her a parcel of books. Day after day she sat with them unopened, staring out at the fields.

It was summer again on a day she was to remember as long as she lived that she set out with the letter the doctor had given her, addressed to a specialist in Winnipeg. It was a short trip, only a few hours, and she had been able to get Bertha in again to look after the children.

The old woman shook her head sadly as she recalled how often on that farm, and how desperately, she had longed to get away, if even for a few hours, to visit the city.

Yet on that afternoon, she had scarcely raised her head as she wandered listlessly around the streets in the vicinity of the railway station.

Once on the corner of Higgins and Main, she had stopped to stare at the people, especially the women and girls, in dresses that barely covered their knees, and with their hair cut so short. They looked so carefree and unrestrained.

As she turned back, a woman coming out of a store

glanced at her and suddenly stopped. Anna hesitated and walked on. Behind her she heard the woman calling her by name. But how? She heard her again and saw her, a city woman, in a short fresh cotton dress and silk stockings, smiling and coming toward her.

"Mrs. Feldesh – Anna –" the woman laughed. "You don't remember me?"

Anna stared at her – a stranger with bright blue eyes and high cheekbones, faintly powered and rouged.

"On the boat!" the woman cried.

Anna stood back. "Even before then," she said at last, very slowly. "In the big waiting shed in Hamburg. You're from Debrecen – You're Mary Németh – Mary." She held out her hands.

They burst into tears and embraced and drew apart and looked at one another.

"I live not far – on Fountain Street," Mary said. "You will come please to – ah, let's talk Hungarian, my God. My husband says I'll never learn."

"So you're married?" Anna said and remembered that Mary was only a few years younger than herself.

The house was not far.

There was the smell of floor wax in the living room and a warm glow of light through the yellow window blinds.

"You talk English so well," Mary said enviously. "But I'm forgetting how to speak Hungarian and I can't really talk English – not even yet. Bill says soon I won't be able to talk at all." She burst into laughter. "He says that's the kind of wife he likes; one who can't talk at all. He's always making fun like that." She looked radiant.

"Bill's English," she added abruptly and flushed. "As soon as we saw each other we knew. Even papa admits – oh, I never told you about papa. When I told mamma I wanted to marry Bill and she told papa, he started to shout and said he'd throw me out of the house.

"You know why he didn't?" Mary asked. "Because even if I was scared, anyway I talked back to him. 'All right,' I said, 'throw me out, but it's not the same here as in the old country. I'll show you.' And I did. I got a job in an overall factory and with overtime I made nearly as much as he did. For two months he never talked to me – not a word. Then one day he said, "All right, enough already with this foolishness. You're getting as thin as a stick in that factory. Tell that Bill of yours he should come and see me."

She clasped her hands tightly in her lap. "Bill's wonderful," she continued, and stopped abruptly and flushed again and sprang to her feet. "But all the time I am talking about me."

Anna rose too. "I must go now," she said.

"But I thought you would stay and have something to eat and see the children," Mary cried. "And Mrs. Geske, you remember? We could go and visit her; she lives only five minutes away."

"I would like to but I have an appointment with a doctor," Anna said.

"With a doctor!" Mary exclaimed. "It's something serious?"

"No – no." She moved to the door. "A backache, that's all. I'm so glad you're happy Mary. It's been so good to see you again."

As she turned to leave she caught a glimpse of herself in a mirror above the chesterfield and for the first time in more years than she could remember really looked at herself, at the forty-year old woman who was staring at her and who looked even more than fifty, upon whose haggard face it seemed she could trace every sorrow she had ever known and in that same instant too as though she had spent all the past years of her life in sleep, wakened and gazed at herself, at those worn and aged features beside this woman's fresh and smiling face and realized it was too late; it was too late to undo what had been done to her.

If she had never come to this country she would never have known. Would that have been better, she wondered, and fiercely shook her head. How could it be better to live like an animal in ignorance? She looked at her face again and it was all she could do to stop herself from weeping.

She scarcely remembered her parting from Mary. They embraced. Once she turned back and waved.

Back on Main Street, she took the letter to the specialist out of her handbag and tore it up.

She remembered Mary's words. "I'll show you," she had said. The words were so childishly inappropriate they were pathetic. Only a few years here in this country and that girl, whom she remembered more clearly now, that shy, timid girl had found the courage to stand up for herself, to take her life into her own hands and make of it what she had determined it should be.

As she continued on her way, she recalled that on the boat she had thought of Mary as a kind and decent girl but in some ways a little silly, too. And yet this woman, silly or not, valued herself, and obviously was held in regard by her husband. And when she stood up to her father, she must have done so with the conviction that she had the right to make her own choice, a right unthinkable in the old country, or if thinkable, then in hope or fantasy.

Anna dried her eyes. All the while she was living with Demetrius, waiting on him hand and foot, cowering every time he raised his arm, working out in the fields like an animal, disregarded in her home, this woman was quietly and happily living her life here in the city, loving and being loved and held in respect.

How could she fail to envy her? This woman had everything and she had nothing. Only a few years separated them – a few years and an abyss, which no matter what happened now, she would never be able to cross.

Dusk was falling when she got to the station; to hold off the thought of reaching home, she fell into a deep stupor that persisted even when she found herself on the silent empty main street of the town.

As she approached the farm, she began to tremble. She walked up the familiar and now hateful path to the house, opened the kitchen door, looked in to see that the children were asleep, and was about to leave when she noticed that the cot which she had set up for Bertha was unoccupied. She had probably gone home after putting the children to bed.

She crossed the narrow hallway to her bedroom, grasped the bedpost to steady herself, and was standing on one foot removing her shoe, when she let it fall from her hand. Demetrius stopped snoring. The girl Bertha, beside him, wakened and sitting up in bed blinked and raised her hands to cover her breasts.

They remained so, looking at one another, then Bertha's right hand moved out and unerringly found hers, Anna's own housecoat, hanging from the nail on the wall.

Anna kicked off her other shoe and ran downstairs, her mind in a turmoil of jubilation and torment, of freedom now at last in sight, and anguish at the recollection of those firm young breasts.

She was in the living room and had already started to pack, folding her linen into her father's great wickerwork trunk, laughing and crying and unable to believe her deliverance should have come so easily, when she saw the girl again standing barefooted in the doorway.

Anna rose from her knees and faced her. "All the time" she said, "when I was sick and sleeping down here, you and my husband . . ." She stopped. It was the measure of the change in her that if she had discovered this between them only yesterday she would have crept into a corner and wept.

The girl seemed suddenly to fall into the room. Behind her Demetrius, in his night shirt, came in and seeing the open trunk, looked, Anna observed, not to her for an answer, but to the girl.

"She knows," Bertha said. "She's going."

"Yes," Anna nodded and smiled. Tomorrow night, somewhere, it didn't matter where, she would be sleeping alone in Winnipeg with the children.

She felt as though her body sang at the prospect of being free of him, and in the same moment, felt she could have torn her housecoat from that strumpet's shoulders and beaten her unmercifully. She noticed that Demetrius was avoiding her eyes. He turned abruptly and pushing the girl out of the room, followed her upstairs.

The old woman paused at Olafson's, the photographer, on Laura Avenue. A few more steps and she would be home. In Olafson's front window were samples of his work and in the very centre stood the picture of little Helena, her granddaughter, the girl she had so long expected and so eagerly yearned for.

"So alright," she said. "For me it was anyway too late."

But it was worth it, the heartache and the drudgery and the long hard weary years. Her eyes shone.

As she stood there it seemed to her that through this bright and lovely child, through this granddaughter of hers, she would be able, more perfectly even then through her daughters, to live the complete life of a free woman here, and grow with her, and see through those clear young eyes what daily unfolded, and awaken to young womanhood again and so bring the sad shattered fragments of her life together once more and become a whole person again.

She smiled and walked on, glad to be reaching home at last.

MARINA MEZEY MCDOUGALL

The Echo Princess

Long ago, when mountains were made out of glass and fairies and people lived together in harmony, there was a fairy king who had three daughters. They lived in an enchanted palace by a lake. The two older sisters grew up to be beautiful fairies and soon they were married and settled in palaces of their own. But the youngest fairy princess, Tihany, the loveliest of the three with her golden hair and deep violet eyes, stayed at home. She had no voice and she could not speak.

Every morning she herded her father's golden-haired goats out to the emerald green pasture and every evening she led them to the sapphire lake. While the goats drank, she sat on her favourite pink quartz rock and gazed at the water, admiring her own reflection. Her face was as lovely as the sunset, but – sad to say – her heart was as hard as diamond.

One evening, as she smiled and made pretty faces at herself in the lake-mirror, the water trembled until she could no longer see her reflection. Her face puckered into a frown as a bearded head wearing a crown emerged from the water.

"I am the King of Waters," said the apparition. "Please, Tihany, fill this silver bucket with milk from your enchanted goats. My son, Balaton, is very ill and nothing can cure him except the milk of the golden-haired goats."

Tihany shook her head impatiently. She wanted the King to go away so she could go on admiring herself.

"If my son cannot have the goat's milk by tonight, he will die," said the King of the Waters. "I beg you, Tihany," added the old King, bowing his white head before the heartless princess.

But Tihany only shook her head again, this time stamping her pretty foot.

"Then I will make a bargain with you," said the King in a hard voice. "If you milk the goats for me, I will give you your voice back."

When she heard that, Tihany smiled her most beautiful smile and jumped to her feet. She took the silver bucket, filled it in the blink of an eye with enchanted goat's milk, and handed it to the King of the Waters with a pretty curtsey. As he took the bucket from her, the King lifted a goldfish out of the lake and gave it to Tihany.

"Swallow this," he commanded. Then he sprinkled magic seaweed and pearls on Tihany's golden hair and said, "When you feel the goldfish tickling your throat you will be able to speak." Then he turned and rode away on the crest of three gigantic waves towards the middle of the lake.

When Tihany could no longer see the King of the Waters in the distance, she felt a little tickle in her throat. She took a deep breath, opened her mouth and out came the most beautiful tinkling voice that anyone has ever heard.

Every evening from that day on Tihany sang beautiful songs to her reflection, while sitting on the pink quartz rock. Her sweet voice travelled along the water and soon everyone who lived by the lake came out in the evenings to listen to her singing. Her fame spread and people came from far and wide to hear her.

Young Prince Balaton rose to the surface of the lake every evening to listen to her. His eyes grew dreamier each day.

"You would be foolish to fall in love with Tihany, my son," warned the King of the Waters, gravely shaking his head. "She has a face as beautiful as the sunset and a voice as sweet as a nightingale's, but her heart is made of hard diamond. She will not return your love."

But young Prince Balaton had already lost his heart.

"Sing me a song, Tihany," he would plead. "Sing to me about love."

"I sing for no one except myself," replied Tihany. Then she added with a laugh, "But I will sing you anything you please if you bring me a gift. Bring me a giant conch full of pearls."

Prince Balaton descended to his underwater palace of seaweed, pearl shells and foam. He filled a smooth pink conch with pearls and swam to the pink quartz rock. Then he placed his offering at Tihany's feet and looked up at her. She smiled at him over the pearls and started to sing a sweet love song. Balaton brought her a gift of pearls every day after that just so he could listen to her sing in her beautiful voice about how much she loved him. After a while he almost came to believe the words of the song, forgetting that he had paid for them.

The young prince was not the only customer.

"Sing us a lullaby, Tihany," asked the little elves who worked in the vineyards of Badacsony, the Wine Mountain.

"You know my price," smiled Tihany. "Bring me a basket of amethysts. Then you will have your lullaby."

The priest from the nearby village went to see her one day.

"With a voice as beautiful as that," he said, "you should praise God."

"If God wants me to sing his praises," answered the selfish princess, "let him send me a dress embroidered with diamond droplets and angel's hair."

And so Tihany continued to live for herself, smile at herself, and sing to herself only. The days passed. Then one evening Prince Balaton did not appear with his gift. Instead,

Tihany saw the old King of the Waters come hurtling towards her on the crest of three gigantic waves.

"My son Balaton is ill," he said. "He will not live very long. Sing into his magic box, Tihany, so I can take your song down to his bedside."

"But where are your treasures?" Tihany asked. "You know that I only sing for payment!"

"My son has already brought you all my treasure," the King thundered, "and we have nothing more to give. Balaton is dying of broken heart because of you. He loves you but he knows he cannot hear you sing again because he has nothing left to bring you as a gift."

Tihany shook her head. "If you do not pay me, I will not sing. Why should I waste a song on someone who is so poor that he has nothing to give me?"

"Have you forgotten how powerful I am?" shouted the King of Waters, trembling with anger. "Have you forgotten how you got your lovely voice?"

"No, I haven't forgotten," answered Tihany. "You gave me my voice to save your son. But now I have all your treasure as well." She looked into the sad eyes of the old King and said with a cold smile, "Without your treasures you are nothing." Then, turning on her heels, she went back to her golden goats.

The King of the Waters disappeared in the angry green waves and a terrible storm raged over the lake for three days and three nights. On the fourth morning the waves were a calm blue once more. There was not even a ripple on the smooth surface.

"Prince Balaton is dead," whispered the goldfish to the seagulls.

"Prince Balaton is dead," whispered the seagulls to the elves.

Soon everyone heard the sad news and everyone mourned for the handsome young prince. People shook their heads at Tihany and no one asked her to sing again. The King of the Waters buried his son in the heart of the Wine Mountain, and the elves, to show their sorrow, molded the whole mountain into the shape of a coffin.

Then the powerful King of the Waters turned his anger into a terrible revenge. Where the lake had been as smooth as a mirror before, it was now constantly raging with storm and there was not a moment's lull when someone could look into the water and see his own reflection. One evening, when Tihany brought her goats to the water, an enormous wave swept the whole herd into the lake until the last golden goat was sucked down to the bottom of a boiling whirlpool.

Tihany, terrified, ran into the nearest cave to escape the angry King of the Waters. But he followed her and rolled a huge stone into the mouth of the cave so that the entrance was completely sealed off from the outside world. With a last pounding of his fists, he uttered this terrible curse:

"I have always kept my word and what I have given you I will not take back. But, in punishment for your selfish greed, you will live in this cave forever and, if anyone should ever speak to you, you will repeat every word seven times!"

The glass mountains have turned into the green hills since then and fairies no longer inhabit the earth. But if you visit Lake Balaton in Hungary you will still find goat-hoof pebbles on the lakeshore after a storm. Those are the hooves of the golden goats, turned to stone. Mount Badacsony has kept the shape of a coffin to this day and its slopes are still covered with vineyards. And, if you wonder through the forests of Tihany, you will find a certain spot where you can stand and shout anything you please and an echo will faithfully repeat your words — exactly seven times — before they dissolve in the sad murmur of the foaming waves.

JOHN MISKA

General Confession

Joe Telekes often spent the cigarette-breaks between classes in the lower lobby of the library with his Grace, György Papp, Archdeacon of the Canadian-Hungarian Greek Catholic Church. Uncle Gyurka was how the faithful fondly styled the white-haired priest, who was born in the same district as Joe, in Nyirgelse, and came to Canada in 1949. After his arrival the church authorities had given him a vicarage in Hamilton, Ontario. During his long service he established congregations in Montreal, Welland, and Courtland in the tobacco-growing region of Western Ontario. In this latter parish, Uncle Gyurka's nephew István Bodnár born in Penészlek into a large family which gave many young men to the church was now the priest. Joe often turned up at their vicarages for social calls, and later for official visits.

During these years, Uncle Gyurka was working on a book on Plato and was doing research at McMaster University's Mills Memorial Library. In one corner the priest had a more-or-less reserved table covered with rows of old editions of Greek, Latin, English and German reference works. With scholarly diligence he took notes from hand-bound dissertations and box-files of archival documents.

The priest and the student, huddled there in the corner in front of the great pile of references, talked away the time with memories of their homeland. At home, people were worried about the harshness of the political regime following the 1956 uprising, the daily revenges and executions. The archdeacon inquired about Joe's father, who, in the wake of the Second World War, had been president of the majority Independent Smallholders' Party in the village. Uncle

Gyurka, at the same time, was a member of parliament representing the same Party. He was a modest man of few words. His whole being radiated the fact that he had been, even in this faraway land, a born village priest.

György Papp has completed his theological studies in Esztergom, read law in Budapest and received his doctorate in canon law. Soon after, he continued his studies in Rome at the Papal Law Institute. Following his return home from Rome he took the position of diocesan canon-law secretary to the Greek Catholic bishop.

Years later, for his achievements in Canada, Pope John XXII conferred upon him the title of Papal Prelate, and Bishop Izidor Boreczki bestowed upon Uncle Gyurka's head the bishop's mitre.

Joseph Telekes was a refugee student from the 1956 Hungarian revolution, and found himself studying fourth-year biology at McMaster. A one-time Baptist denominational institution, the university in Hamilton gave twenty-two Hungarian students refuge, and placed them in private homes. Language courses were hastily organized at a nearby high school. After passing exhaustive entrance examinations, five of their number were accepted for chemistry and biology and for courses in the humanities. The students, after overcoming the initial difficulties, did quite well. Two went onto post-doctoral studies in chemistry at American universities and became renowned scientists in their field.

Joe Telekes was an honours student. One of his essays on the effects of the x-chromosome on human longevity was published by the Ottawa-based Canadian Journal of Biological Sciences, a rare achievement in Canadian student life.

In the week preceding graduation, Joe mentioned to Uncle Gyurka that he would much like to come to make his confession before leaving for Toronto to pursue his graduate studies. "By all means," said the archdeacon, while flicking ash from his Export-A cigarette into an old pedestal ashtray. "Come in Sunday morning before the holy liturgy."

Joe Telekes kept his appointment with Uncle Gyurka and God.

The church was on James Street in the Hungarian neighbourhood in the centre of town. Nearby were the storefronts of Kutz travel agents, a Hungarian butcher shop and the Budapest Restaurant where, if truth be told, Joe and his schoolmates turned up more often than in Uncle Gyurka's church!

Its faded front, built amongst improbable companions, betrayed the church's working-class background: Uncle Gyurka had bought it from the Civic Workers' Union. The renovations on the building's extensive hall had been done by members of the congregation. They raised a small dais for the altar, put backless benches in the main area for the faithful and the two cantors, indeed there were two, and close to the entrance, an armchair outfitted with a small table. The budget did not allow for the gilded icons that should have been there. No frescoes of the saints graced the cream-coloured walls. The Hamiltonians didn't want to spend too much on the exterior either. They were dreaming of a new, onion-shaped steeple, similar to the ones that dominated the villages in the old country. A decade later, with contributions from the congregation and the diocese, they did build a beautiful church.

With a lump in his throat, the penitent knelt down in front of Uncle Gyurka's chair. The archdeacon placed the confessional shawl over Joe's head and asked, "When did you confess last?"

"Seven years ago," came the halting answer.

After a short pause, the priest said, "Then it will be a general confession."

It was.

After he left his village for the gimnázium at Hajd-böszörmény, he did go to church from time to time to confess and to worship. With the passing years, however, he had imbibed the materialist ideas of the time and thought less and less of following the practices of spiritual life. Quietly, with genuine sorrow, he listed his sins. God knows, there were plenty of them. For example, he had failed to observe the days of fast, neglected to pray every day, had not always honoured his superiors, especially unprincipled politicians. Then he thanked God for helping him in this alien land, despite his transgressions.

Following this confession, Uncle Gyurka placed his hand on top of Joe's head and explained the transcendence of purity of soul over the vulnerability of the carnal body. Then, with understanding words, absolved Joe of his sins. "Go in peace, and sin no more!" he said, after he gave the young man the penance he should perform.

With bowed head and hands clasped before him, Joe withdrew to the last row of benches and knelt to pray. The members of the congregation began to arrive, whispering over the sound of their shuffling feet, nodding to each other in greeting.

Hardly had he finished the prescribed penance when the liturgy of the holy mass began.

The assistant had helped Uncle Gyurka don the white-laced alb, called sztiharion by the Greek Catholics, and the epitrachelion, a long stole with its seven equilimbed Greek crosses representing the Seven Sainthoods. He had then given the priest the heavy, tasselled cincture to tie around his waist. This was followed by the embroidered cuffs for his wrists, and finally the richly adorned felon, or chasuble, was guided over the celebrant's head, so that the servant of God be mantled as he should.

Holding the Holy Book high before him, the archdeacon proceeded to the front of the altar and began the ceremony. It came upon Joe that Uncle Gyurka was uttering the words of the mass in the voice of everyday conversation. In the past, at home, Father István Sebella's reverent lips had pronounced a veritable symphony of oblations compared to this mundane recitation. In place of high-flying oratory, Gyurka's homily as well developed its theme with the methodical dryness of a low-key academic essay.

The subject, though, was abiding interest to his congregation: the history of the Greek Catholic faith. György Papp told the assembled that the United Denominations would be a more accurate name, since besides the Greeks a number of other nationalities in Eastern Europe had worshipped according to the same ancient dogmas of faith. Before the Magyar occupation of the Carpathian Basin in A.D. 896, the Byzantine faithful had taught and converted those who lived in the region Czechs, Serbs, Ruthenians, Macedonians, Romanians. Among the occupying Magyars there were also a number of Old Christians, Prince Géza among them. New research indicates, explained Uncle Gyurka, that in the Kiev area, Prince Árpád's father, Álmos, already had been involved in spreading Christianity. King Steven, principally for political and military reasons, was led to grant favour to the Roman variant of the Christian creed.

"In his continuing tolerance of the Eastern Rite, one may see the wisdom of our King Saint Steven," Uncle George emphasized.

He elaborated further that the name Greek Catholic is the result of a temporary union between Rome and the Byzantine Patriarchy achieved at the Council of Florence in 1438. This was done in hope of aiding the West against

Ottoman expansion. The Hungarian Greek Catholics joined them in 1646, and at the same time were doing their best to replace Old Slav and Old Greek with the Magyar language in the practice of their rite. This undertaking in face of Rome's resistance took a hundred years to succeed. Only then could the priests of Hungary legitimately sing their more beautiful than beautiful hymns in their native tongue.

Despite the distance in long years, Joe remembered well his participation in the mass. Now, he sang the hymns with the forty or so faithful gathered here.

As I have said, there were two cantors, one young, the other older. The first was well dressed, and sang from a hymnal, clearly enunciating the phonetics of even the most familiar songs. Each syllable precisely followed the last, carefully observing the extensions called for by musical phrasing . . . Ho-ly Mo-ther of Go-od.

At midpoint of the mass, the elder cantor started to lose control of himself. His responses to the celebrant became ever louder. The veins on his neck and forehead stood out. He rushed the start of verses, not even waiting for Uncle Gyurka to finish his. This great enthusiasm brought on a coughing fit. At first it came in short volleys that he tried to clear with unintelligible grunts; then, as soon as he opened his mouth for another song, came a full barrage. His face turned beet red, his eyes bulged. A middle-aged, doll-faced lady, probably his wife, toddled up to him from her place in the front pew, placed her hand on his and whispered something in his ear. The white-haired cantor nodded, and abandoned singing.

From this point, the brewing tension in the church fastened its grip more tightly on the congregation. Those who came from the hamlets of Eastern Hungary, ill-schooled in the flow of the liturgy, became completely confused. The hymns grew so muted that not even in front of the church, out on the sidewalk at the steps, could a passerby have heard how those within were praising the glory of God in High Mass.

On his way home, to the accompaniment of the shakes and rattles of the King Street bus, Joe's memory rang with the memory of the old-country church, its Eastern pomp and penoplied sound.

There a wonderfully gilded iconostasis separated the equally gilded tabernacle from the nave. There were three doors in the iconostasis; through the centre door only an ordained priest had the right to enter. The walls and ceilings of the church had filled him with wonder, as a child, at the frescoes depicting the mysteries of the faith there. A thousand worshippers could find a place within the great nave and the drafty God's Acre of the old church. The schoolchildren were ranked in front, girls on the right, boys to their left. Alongside in high-backed arm-chairs sat and sometimes slept the more well-to-do farm owners.

Behind the schoolchildren stood the students from the higher grades. The young wives, hair tied with flowery kerchiefs, stood next behind. In the transepts and the room for the infirm, the elderly thronged together in their black attire. The bachelor young men, hair shining with walnut oil, were up in the choir loft with the cantor. They, with the young wives were the soul of the congregation. At summer high masses like this one, when the doors and windows were left wide open and the churchyard too was crowded with the faithful, the hymns could be heard by those living in the next village, let alone those passing by on the sidewalk, especially the Sanctus, marking the mid-point of the mass:

Holy, holy, ho-ly Lord God of the multitudes,
Heaven and Earth are filled with Thy glory,

Hosanna-a-a in the hights of Heaven,
Blessed is He who comes in the name of the Lord,
Hosanna in the heights of Heaven.

At home the student locked the door. Thanks to the kindness
of the Archdeacon Uncle Gyurka, Joe Telekes had got away
with three Our Father's, three Hail Marys, and the custom-
ary Mea Culpas whispered from the depth of his heart as
penance for his errors. He prayed and began to cry.

GEORGE PAYERLE

London Scenes

Regent Street at the evening rush hour gathers him into the tide-change human sea going up from Piccadilly and down from Oxford Circus. It seems everyone in London is pouring through that stately curve fronted with amber stone buildings that make him dizzy following their unbroken sweep against the sky. People and buses, cabs and bicycles elbow to fender from one wall to the other, moving in oceanic time, carry him along as though he too had purpose. He brushes the sleeve of a cyclist in a bowler hat, brolly strapped to his machine, and is brushed by the arm of a woman whose tailored shoulders and brisk bottom march into the throng of backs and fronts before him. He eddies into the lee of a columned entrance and leans against the smooth square bulk of its abutment. The stone feels warm. He looks at them all coming toward him. In the heart of an army of ten million. A nation city. They round from a perfect arc he'd followed into this straight gut of Regent Street. Each one has a face. Old and young, in shirts and skirts and jeans and suits. A woman in a maroon blouse, breasts dancing to the rhythm of her stride, a swatch of skirt just curtaining her loins. He looks at her strong-boned English face and sees his own mirrored in her dark electric eyes. Startled, he nods. Her nod in reply says, Yes, you're here too. It would have been the same if they had both been naked. He feels naked. Not undressed, but as though he were wearing only his skin, touched by everyone. An exquisite gent in a London Fog swirling over his pinstripe suit inclines a handsome chin. They all have faces. A pair of grannies with Liberty's bags, the one with her hand on the other's arm, support each other like frail handrails through the crowd. Good afternoon for tea. A taut youth in white Levi shirt and jeans snug as a codpiece on his well-hung crotch. The faces say, You've seen us. This is how we are.

Sam goes down to Picadilly again for the sheer joy of it. You're welcome here. This is human being. He feels Charlotte's breath in him. You lived here so long, he thinks. And longs for Lily willowing beside him in this dance against death. Breath of our breath, he thinks. What am I saying? All the living and the dead pass by under the grand arced ramparts of Regent Street, like the river of time flowing in both directions. And he turns to go up again.

He finds himself in Liberty's running his fingers through piles of silk. An amber scarf patterned in maroon wraps itself around his hands and slips through them like heavy warm mist.

That night he lies in his bed listening to the presence of London, the scarf clasped to his stomach like a live thing that ebbs and flows with his breath.

With each breath the dark rushes in and out of him and he sees constellations of light burst like pale fires in space, like slow-blossoming tears. The names of Charlotte and Lily and Dot, first Hugh and second Hugh and Nancy, Braithwaite and Fred and even his own. Each life tangible as the breath in his body, full and round and warm and fleeting as starlight on the water at Tuckenhay as the swans sail into his sleep, sound of his breath and sound of London indistinguishable as dreams.

He wraps the scarf around her hands and clasps his own over them.

"I got you this because it feels nice," he says. The silk warmer than her skin on his.

"Sam, it's lovely," she says. They look at each other and the tears welling in each other's eyes. Charlotte leans up from her bed and he holds her sobs against his, afraid she might slip away and be gone like an armful of feathers.

But Charlotte's arms are strong around his neck and she pulls herself straight. "Fine pair of hydrants we are," she says and blows her nose.

"Yeah," he grins, wetly.

Her hand with the scarf in it reaches out to stroke his hair. "It's so good to have you here, Sam." Her eyes make little quick movements, twin birds taking in all of his face, all of him.

"You're not afraid of death the way the others are."

"Charlotte, coming here I was terrified. But you made me so damn happy . . ." He shrugs. "I feel like I'm good for something and I'm not used to that."

She laughs. "You certainly are good for something, Sam. You mustn't think badly of yourself. It's such a boon to know that you'll be here when I'm gone." She's trying to say something too and not knowing how. He thinks of Regent Street. How do you say these things?

"You'll always be here, Charlotte." He waves his arm and looks out the window. "You're part of this place."

He turns back to her and sees her eyes seeing London and time.

"What have I done with my life?" she says. Lottie. "All that paper. I've made showers of paper fly. And known a few people as far as their skins. My friend Fran has such lovely ivory skin. A few men. The wet frantic things that bodies do. Is that what we have done? A paper blizzard falling all over Britain and half the world. And in the dark some dripping bodies. A few noble faces. Glimpses of urchins in the streets and fat fruit vendors. Sunlight on St Paul's . . ."

"Lottie, you've helped people all over the world –"

"And what good's that if you hardly know the ones next to you?"

"Look at me. I fought in a war and turned into a drunk."

"You don't look like much of a drunk to me, Sam. You came all this way so I could have someone close to me. There's no one here I could talk to this way."

"Maybe you're right." He grins. "I never really made it as a drunk. It just seems like a good excuse."

She looks suddenly startled. "Where are you staying? I never thought to ask."

"Up in that hotel in Bayswater you found me last time."

"But you stay in the flat!"

"I checked with the Arab and he said you'd asked them to close it up, whatever that means."

"Oh dear, yes. You see I haven't known what to do. I thought to leave almost everything to the organization – the Red Cross, you know – with something for Hugh and Carol," she smiles, "and you. But until the time really came . . . At any rate, I'll instruct Hartnell's to open it up again for you. You know, he said they could rent it as an Arab flat and it would earn heaps of money. Why do you think an Arab would say a thing like that?"

"Because he's a London Arab and the others are foreign Arabs. Look L., it's okay. The Garden Court is cheap enough."

She looks at him speculatively. She's half daft, he thinks. Seeping away, her life, like water in sand. The scarf plays in her fingers like fluid gold and dark blood.

"What have you been doing, Sam? Have you work? I had a report from Dot but I think I dragged it out of her, it was that skimpy. Poor Dot. What will you do when you go back? When this is. . . done?"

He takes her hand again. The silk and the pasty skin. "It's been pretty much the same since the heart attack," he says. "Odd jobs and holing up in my rooms when I'm not in a bar. But like you said about the booze, I think it's time I got a proper job. Hugh's Nancy said I should be a commissionaire, and maybe the wench is right."

"Oh dear, that doesn't sound much like you, in one of those stiff uniforms. But I'm glad you've seen Hugh and Nancy. Is she nice?"

"She's wonderful."

The speculative look returns. "Sam," she says, "you've always wanted to live in England, haven't you? Why don't I leave the property to you? John Jameson's managing the cottage in Totnes and he's to be executor. You liked John, I think, didn't you? There's quite a bit of money, and the rentals. You could live in whichever place you choose, or sell one . . ."

"Lottie," he says, "No. I'm just one guy. The Red Cross . . ." He shrugs. "Don't upset everything you planned just because I showed up out of nowhere."

"I'm not so sure," she says. "They had most of my life." She looks at him as though she were seeing a place to go. "You don't have very much to show for what you gave us all. And you've given me my family back when I needed it most." He can feel her in him like a pressure testing the rightness of things. Like an embrace. A particularization of London. He feels at once frightened and comforted.

He puts his hands on her shoulders and leans over to kiss her on the forehead.

"I think it's right the way it is, L.," he says. "Let it lie. You should rest."

"You could always decide when it's your turn to go," she says, like someone who has seen a truth. She smiles and holds up the scarf. "It's like marigolds," she says, "made of marigolds," and closes her eyes.

In Leicester Square it's Sunday. The people who visit mingle with the people who live there, pigeon-feeders strewing their crumbs among the sleeping figures scattered like bundles of old clothing on the lawns and benches like corpses. He stands by the stairs leading down to the public loos, gazing at the Ritz and Empire and Odeon across the way. One marquee shows a sere yellow picture of rolling grassland loomed over by the giant figures of the Hollywood heroes, the old and the young. A film he'd thought to see in Victoria before it got away. The other side of the world. Those film-houses make a horizon. Beyond them, invisible as prairie beyond the next rise, more buildings, more streets, squares, gardens, greens. If I walked for a day I couldn't walk out of this place, he thinks.

"All right?" a parade-ground voice booms. Its owner big as a wall. Sam startles like a fish in his skin. A Guardsman, no doubt, ginger moustaches flaring over a beefy red visage no younger than his own. He remembers the answer.

"All right," he says.

"Smashing! Can't be all that gloomy, what?" A shooting stick and cap. Sam grins, feeling feeble but befriended.

"Chin up then, there's a good lad!" the giant shouts, giving him a comfortable whack on the bottom with his stick. "March on! March on!" and marches down into Leicester Square, a broad tweed-jacketed back implacably plunging amongst the pigeons feathered and clothed there.

Sam takes a breath and descends the steps to piss. Mosaic Hogarth in the stairwell. Down there, electric light gleams on porcelain and tile and glows in the varnished years of the wooden cubicles. The bath attendant, towel on arm, chats with a pair of gentlemen hippies in expensive boots and suede-look denim. Sam makes water in the men's clubroom at Leicester Square.

The National Gallery closed for improvements. The pubs not open. Charlotte more or less in a coma. You call this life? he says to the mirror. What sorta bullshit you tryin' ta hand me?

The mirror says March on, you old fart, and Hogarth says the same on the way back up the stairs. He considers the Tate but can't face the chance of more Sunday improvements. The day, after all, ain't gloomy. A sort of yellowish dusty promise of rain that could mean anything in this town. Kew, he thinks. That other Charlotte's garden. And goes to find a train.

Having exchanged dour glances with the collector of ha'pennies at the gate, having marvelled at the stacks of the wee coins on his table and what it must cost her Majesty's taxpayers to collect them, Sam crunches along gravel paths the pagoda – closed for structural reasons – and the structurally impeccable spar tree presented by the people of British Columbia as a kind of wooden send-up to Cleopatra's Needle. The trees of Kew, living and dead, come from everyplace to stand at spacious intervals as monuments to botany.

The growth thickens until he is in a forest. In the forest stands Queen Charlotte's Cottage, closed up because this is not a special occasion. No hunting parties from Westminster closeted there so the royals can get pissed by a resinous fire. No Charlotte. The day chills as it wanes.

Further along he leans on a gate separating the gardens from the Thames embankment. A slightly more bucolic Thames. The sky looks like yellow, varnished silver and makes the river glow as it slides beneath the bright acid green foliage along the near bank. The eerie brown lustrous water carries phantasms of baroque barges past his eyes and the chill wind rings in his ears like tarnished brass.

The place at Kew would like to close because the hour is late but he buys his ticket and treads where the carpets lead him over bare wood floors to the chair in which Queen Charlotte died. He looks at the worn black upholstery and imagines he hears it creak as the frail body settles into it one last time, eyes if they see gazing out that window over Thames. Hears it creak again as the body is lifted out, heavier by the life that's gone. The light from the window. What others have sat here since? Hurry up, please, the palace is closing. Charlotte's islands, wilderness west of wilderness, that belong still to the ravens and the eyes of Charlie Eden-shaw.

The greenhouses are closed because the tour is late. The coldframes in this botanical garden of the Gardens are closed because they are coldframes. He wanders into trellised acres that look like winter. One man forlorn with his barrow tends a bed that must simply be of another season but seems like everything around it a ruined estate. A survivor, he thinks, grubs for roots. *Gone with the Wind* on the eve of blitz-krieg.

Toward the duck pond toward sunset, pampas grasses and strange fleshy little plants from Siberia. Stone beasts of heraldry guard the Victorian glass marquee of the tropical house. Inside, palm trees scrape the high ceiling, a south-seas silhouette against the wintry sun. He shivers. The pewter scrollwork sky says it won't be summer again today. A flotilla of Canada Geese show the flag to the ducks, sailing past the stone bestiary and its empty row of graceful wooden benches. Each has a little brass plaque. In loving memory of Mavis and the happy hours.

On the east side of the pond he peers through windows of someone's mansion that has become a museum of agriculture. The history of potatoes and corn displayed in glass cases. He remembers the lone gardener. I have loved you long and silently, he says, fondling tubers out of warm earth. The maize winks its red and yellow eyes in the crystal sunset shining through the palm trees.

SZABOLCS SAJGÓ

an entreaty

if we flow like rivers on a planet without oceans
to cascade roarless into the void at the world's edge
and choke like eager tempests flung into caves
Lord have mercy
if we blaze like home fires hearthed on glacial peaks
or birds alone in an empty sky
as sorrow derided in the midst of laughter
Lord have mercy
if we fear malice in every approaching step
and see sharp teeth in every smile
if we shudder at every sound
Lord have mercy
if we mournfully gaze at the stars
as though they were flickering hearths
seen from afar in alien homes
Lord have mercy
if we are the she-wolf licking her butchered young
the nesting bird falling in the felled tree
spawning fish in dead oceans
Lord have mercy
if we envy the rooted trees
and flowers that bloom with the fleeting sunlight
the wild geese migrating over the sea
Lord have mercy
if we hang Van Gogh's paintings on blind men's walls
and trumpet Beethoven to the deaf
if we are the word preached in an empty church
Lord have mercy
that we may not keep the peace of volcanoes
nor pleasure whores

nor soundproof the torture chambers
Lord have mercy

Translated by George Payerle

from the focus of drawn bows

furtive in ripe beauty while younger sisters slept
how many desires rode arousal's waves
along the secret winding ways of your mother's sanctuary
to welcome entry, to await excitedly in their nest-warm
     space
the rosy sweat-drenched opening of life's door round
that the hot hard cabriolet might gallop in
from somewhere beyond forest and hills
and pour forth an army led victorious into the seed-core
at the reddening apple's heart
where would come to rest
in cooling convulsions of the life-tree
its seducer
the lascivious future's snake
how many desires prepared in vain
how many washed away
by floods of blood tossed into a soiled grave

and how often in lonely outcast evenings
did a bold dream of joy toil-weary by hearthlight
and errant thoughts in a cold bed
raddle of the heart's young longing
a myriad restless writhing
in your father's secret workplace
where storerooms filled to bursting
that along blood-rich roads
desire might lay siege

and breach its prison walls
but how often did it flow away in confused dreams by night
or the blaze of phantasmal days
or freeze stranded on the hills
in the wilderness of coupling
barred from the carmine cave's warmth
too weak to get over the dams
or simply left standing in the footrace
when the tight hot gunmuzzle fired onto the battlefield
how many victorious urges snaked in vain
because the bewitching Eden-woman they imagined
in no way waited with proferred loins
but made ready still in her dark cell
or withered past her bloom

how many desires chased each other so long in vain
until at last in the untiring focus of two tightly drawn bows
you took form for your uncertain flight
you rainbow-dream of watery skies
you earthly face abandoned here
you briefly enduring encounter of two worlds

Translated by George Payerle and Karl Sandor

ANNA PORTER

The Storyteller
(Memory, Secrets, Magic and Lies – An Excerpt)

My childhood was filled with my grandfather's stories. Some I remember so clearly, that I still hear his voice in their telling and still see the pictures I saw when I first heard them. My whole family told stories – many true, a few imagined, others invented so long ago they had become true – but none were as full of life as my grandfather's.

There were wise witches and wily giants, magic horses and soothsayers who commanded ancient spells; there were princes and heroes who did battle against the powers of evil; there were grand viziers, and turbaned armies of merciless Turks; and there were our Hungarian ancestors who never tired of wielding their broadswords in defense of our ancient lands. He told stories about glittering dances in bygone courts, and poets whose words could move more people than military commands ever had. There were stories about his three beautiful daughters and their gallant admirers, about his mother who told him her tales until late into the Bácska nights, his grandfather who held court in Transylvania and was murdered at his own dinner table, and about his grandmother, the dark-eyed Petronella who escaped with her young son, then drove her wagon for three days and four nights to arrive at dawn in the tiny village of Kula in the southern Hungarian region of Bácska where my grandfather was born some fifty years later.

He was my childhood hero.

His name was Vili. Actually, his name was Vilmos but everyone called him Vili. He was a big raw-boned man, and even when I came along, and he was well into his fifties, he was extraordinarily strong. He used to demonstrate his strength by doing crazy things like lifting chairs with people sitting on them. To prove that both his arms were equally strong, he sometimes lifted two chairs and two people at once.

He would crouch down between the two chairs, grab one leg in each hand, take a deep breath, puffing up his chest and his cheeks, then lift. His back straight, his eyes focused on some midpoint over our heads, he would slowly stand up. The veins on the sides of his neck and down the centre of his forehead stood out like ropes. All the while the people on the chairs – usually his daughters or their rather temporary boyfriends or husbands – were stiff as statues. Everyone else applauded, and Vili's bald head took an almost imperceptible bow. After that, he'd quickly deposit his charges, rub his big palms together, and wink at his most appreciative audience – me.

He could stop ice-carts by stepping in front of the horses, grabbing the pole between them and pushing back on it, till their front hooves clawed the air; then he'd let them down gently because he did not want to hurt the horses or let the ice-blocks slide off and break. Back in the early fifties, ice still came by horse and cart to Budapest in the summer. On hot days my friends and I would run behind the carts, picking up bits of fallen ice and rubbing them over our faces, or trying to stuff ice shards down each other's shirt fronts. We wrestled and shoved to get the best spots nearest the back wheels, so we could soak in a freezing cold shower when the cart stopped for its deliveries. We got the best showers when my grandfather lifted the front of the cart.

When my grandfather was nineteen he represented Hungary in four events at the European Games. One of them was the shot-put, another the épée. I could never figure how he could shine at both events, seeing that one required a heavy step while carrying something that weighed over sixteen pounds and for the other you had to be light on your feet. For a decade he held the European record in the one-hundred-yard dash. At the 1908 London Olympics, he finished fourth behind three Americans, but he also took part in the pentathlon.

He became, quite accidentally, Hungarian heavyweight wrestling champion for a year. He had been sauntering past the elevated rink in the University Club gym when the try-outs ended. The guys were shouting, "Why don't you get up there, Vili, don't you have the courage to face the champ?" Vili was not from Budapest – he was a landowner's son from the South. A brawny boy. He needed to show he was better than anyone else. That was the only reason he won. The champion didn't have anything to prove.

He played soccer on the Budapest University team and impressed his colleagues with his ability to make the opposing team members laugh. He did magic tricks with the ball; and with his kerchief, and socks. Sometimes he made white pigeons appear from his pockets and let them fly away while his team scored a goal. At my fourth birthday party, he conjured up a white rabbit, a turtle and two miniature pinschers who promptly started yelping and chasing the rabbit around the apartment, much to the delight of my friends and the distress of my grandmother who told him he would have to return all the animals to wherever he'd found them: we were no longer in our own house and could not afford to feed a menagerie.

Sometimes when we travelled on the Rákóczi út streetcar, he'd make forints disappear, or if there were children in the seats across from ours, he'd take the coins out of his pockets – a very respectable, well-dressed, elderly gentleman – examine them, pretend to taste them, then eat them. On our way to the exit, he'd make them reappear from the children's ears, and look most disapproving, surprised that they had somehow taken his repast of coins and hidden them so well. I remember the children's faces, at first embarrassed, then fascinated, then amazed, finally released into laughter when my grandfather stepped off the streetcar, adjusted his pocket handkerchief, and headed off towards one of his favorite coffee houses.

Of all his talents, I think he was proudest of his prowess with the sword.

He had been, arguably, the best swords dueller in Budapest. Mostly, his duels were fought in the early hours, at five or six in the morning, somewhere in a park, Városliget (City Park) for example, where you could barely see your opponent in the dawn fog. Yet a crowd gathered every time Vili Rácz fought. "Vili was a reprobate," his brother told me, pursing his lips as he gazed off into his pálinka-induced stillness. "A skirt-chaser. He should never have fought, knowing he was an Olympic champion, and the others backyard swordsmen. They never had a chance." Fortunately, the duels usually ended after first blood had been drawn.

No one in my home liked to talk about my grandfather's duels. "It's because they were all about women," Béla told me. My first memory of Béla is of him smoking foul-smelling cigars in a tiny apartment full of dark furniture which was not to be sat upon or touched. It was hung with dusty velvet curtains, slimy to my fingers, and musty with age and perspiration, as were his ancient-looking clothes.

Béla had small refined hands, a high forehead and a very red face. He was shorter than my grandfather and drank pálinka – Hungarian plum brandy – only because most of the time nothing else was available. Otherwise, he preferred Calvados. His breath was rancid with garlic, nicotine and alcohol. He said he had once been a very important person in parliament.

When I relayed this information to my grandfather, he said, "Of course," which in my grandfather's language meant, bullshit. But Vili never swore.

Béla was his youngest brother, the boy who leans over his mother's knee in the old photograph Vili had of his parents' young family. All the boys wear the same round-necked white shirts, knee socks and short pants. Vili, the eldest, has his right hand on his hip and looks directly into the camera. Gyula, who later stopped speaking to Vili after their Turkish-baths venture, is gazing at his father. Béla plays with his fingers. Later, he was the one who stayed behind on the family estate, trying to command the farmhands after his father died, and he was the one who failed most spectacularly.

Because I spent most of my childhood trying to impress my grandfather, I took up fencing – I won no medals, and my fondest memory of my fencing days is of a dank, yellow-lit gymnasium and a dozen of us, all pretending we were auditioning for The Three Musketeers. Alexander Dumas' book had been a huge hit in Hungarian and we all knew the stories. We were taught by a Jesuit friend of my grandfather who was somewhat portly and tended to fall asleep during much of the thrust and parry. Unfortunately, he was fully awake the day I discovered I was going to have breasts. I was wearing a white shirt that hung over a pair of loose black shorts down to my knees, more or less like the ones I had seen Vili wear in those old brown and yellow photographs with serrated edges that showed him winning medals against Swedes or Greeks. What with the enthusiastic leaping about I had come to associate with my fencing efforts, I had worked up quite a sweat.

Suddenly I realized that the other kids had begun to

giggle and fidget. I became distracted, dropped my épée, and faced the old Jesuit's face about an inch from my nose. He had missed his chance to pretend-stab me, as he usually did when I missed a step. "Well," he said with not much of a smile on his face, "there are many reasons why girls are no good at this stuff. Two of them are staring at me, and they're not the sort of thing priests are supposed to see. So, how about putting on a sweater?"

The other kids were all boys whose fathers had been in the cavalry during Second World War – or so they claimed. I put on my sweater and swore all the way home. For sons of cavalrymen, I thought, they had seemed rather lacking in chivalry.

Chivalry was an art much discussed in our home back then. Vili was a gentleman of the old ways, with a great fondness for Spencer, Shakespeare, Vörösmarty, Petofi, Gardonyi, Dumas, Jókai, Stendhal, Madács, Dickens, Tolstoy, Arany and a range of Hungarian poets who celebrated chivalry and the sadness of our history in long narrative poems of ringing rhymes and galloping rhythms.

I had dreamt of becoming a great poet-swordsman, and it seemed dreadfully unfair that my ambitions should be dashed by something as insignificant as nipples.

I took up running but showed about as much talent for that as I had shown for fencing. Sometime during the second lap of my first real race, I lost my footing and fell headlong tripping the runner behind. Vili spared us both by not coming to see me in action.

My mother thought my big flapping 1920s bloomers were to blame. They had slid down and the rubber snagged my knees.

My grandfather loved women but knew nothing about women's clothes. His discomfort was surprising, given that by that time he had already fathered three daughters with my grandmother and, though I didn't know about them till much later, some sixteen other children by an assortment of women who had found him irresistible.

His "gallivanting," as his daughter Leah used to call it, created little rivulets of tension around our dinner table. Now and then my grandmother, whose name was Therese, would throw some hot and soggy food at him and they would both leave the table to shout at each other in their (and my) bedroom.

Most of the time, though, my grandmother adored him. She called him Papa and always served his food first. He got the biggest helpings.

My grandmother had once been a stunningly beautiful girl, with lush black hair, a small oval face, high forehead, and big olive-black eyes. She was slender and small, maybe five foot one to his six foot two, her head reaching my grandfather's chest "around heart level," as he'd tell us. When the two of them walked together, she seemed fragile and insubstantial.

She came from a village in what is now Slovakia, but back then, and for hundreds of years before, it was called Upper Danubia, and was a part of Hungary. She and Vili met in one of the few spaces in Hungarian history when the country wasn't at war, or occupied by marauding armies, or just marauding citizens, from elsewhere.

For centuries Hungary had provided a barrier of live folk between opposing factions of Slavs and Germans, a major accomplishment that helped focus the German tribes into one coherent nation and stopped the westward expansion of unwanted easterners such as the Tatars and the Turks, each of whom slaughtered Hungarians for sport over several centuries.

We had a photograph of Therese taken when she was sixteen and almost a bride. A formal portrait, it was commissioned by her parents just before she was carried off by the Transylvanian giant. The picture is tinted light brown. She has glowing eyes in a pale face. Her nose is small, there is a tiny dimple in her chin. She has an uncertain smile. Her long hair is gathered at the nape of her neck and fastened with a white ribbon. Her shoulders are bare. When I asked if that was not too daring for the times, she told me the dress had been painted out by the photographer, but I didn't believe her.

There are various stories about how they met.

In one of them, she is walking home by the side of the road, carrying a basket of flowers. ("Why is she carrying flowers?" "Shhh . . . it's the way the story goes.") He passes by in an open carriage. He has just arrived by train from Budapest for a weekend shooting party at a friend's country estate and he is in a hurry, he wants to be there for the festive dinner. But he tells the coachman to stop when he sees her. He thinks her waist is impossibly small, her ankles exquisite, her hair too thick and unruly for the ribbons. She is wearing a blue and red skirt and white embroidered blouse.

The air is heavy with the scent of white acacia blossoms.

"We are going in the same direction," he tells her, "I would be deeply honoured if you would allow me to take you." Hungarian was a very formal language back then.

At first she demurs. "How do you know it's the same direction?" Her eyes are lowered but through the dark fringes of her lashes, she sees his smile.

He jumps from the carriage into the dust of the road and she notices for the first time how tall he is. His shoulders strain against the fine wool fiber of his black jacket. The collar of his white linen shirt is hand-stitched. Everything he wears is expensive, down to the soft black leather boots gleaming with spit and polish.

"Wherever you go is the right direction," he says.

When he lifts her into the carriage the tips of his fingers touch at her back as his big hands encircle her slender waist. She blushes when he tells her she's the prettiest girl in Upper Danubia.

Forty years later he was still telling her she was the prettiest woman in Upper Danubia, and she still believed him.

In another version, my grandmother is helping to serve the guests in a huge house close to my great-grandfather's ancestral home in Erdély. She is a friend of the host's young daughter. When she ladles the stag broth into his Herendi porcelain bowl Vili catches her hand.

My great-great-grandfather had sat in a similar room, at another long oak dining table, dressed for the evening in maroon velvet jacket with gold braid, when he was shot through the window by an unhappy Wallach. My great-great-grandfather's blood soaked into the floorboards at the head of the oak table where he sat for his evening meals, and it is still there. According to Vili.

Vili holds my grandmother's hand gently, turns it to kiss the first knuckle of her little finger, then returns it, as if it were a gift. She hesitates, feels herself blush, her lips tremble. There is laughter around the table.

She is sure they are laughing at her embarrassment. Years later, he still insists they were laughing at a joke about a Wallachian hunting party where the only one left standing at the end of the day is the stag. No one had noticed his holding her hand.

He tells the joke again to his friends at the Százéves, where he often took me for pretzels and beer. There are cardboard squares under the fluted beer glasses, the long dark wood tables are stained with beer. Men in black suits with white shirts play gypsy music. No one has money to tip them. And he tells the story again in the Emke coffee house where he plays chess in the window with other friends, and sometimes by himself. A crowd gathers wherever he goes. The head waiter bows, though he only gives him a forint, not enough for a single cigarette. Even that, he is reluctant to accept and often slips it into my hand.

His friends exchange gossip about politics using chess codewords even I can understand. "Don't let the pawns get your knight, Vili."

"Watch your back when you cross the rook."

Every time he tells the stag story everybody laughs.

Later, when he told the story in New Zealand, in his too-formal English, nobody did.

In my aunt Leah's version of my grandparents' courtship, Vili met Therese at the Pozsony ball. She was poor gentry, but her parents had saved for a gown of white muslin and silk so their youngest daughter could one day attend the debutantes' ball. It was the beginning of the season, the girls wore long white gloves, silk-covered shoes, rosebuds in their hair. The sons of the gentry would come to the first ball to see the new crop of girls. Vili chose the best of the lot, my grandmother.

"Like a goose market?" I asked.

Leah gave this some thought. "A little," she agreed, smiling.

When Vili and Therese married, they moved into a house on the classy side of the river Danube, Buda. He spoilt her with expensive jewellery, flowers that came in giant Chinese vases, and servants to attend to her wishes. He had promised her family he would care for her always. Or so he told me.

But by the time of my first clear memories, we lived on the other side of the Danube, Pest, in a cramped apartment overlooking the streetcar tracks and the flashing neon lights of Pest's biggest department store. There were no more servants, and my grandmother had taught herself to cook and wash dishes.

My grandmother rarely complained about what she had lost. She kept a few mementoes, pretty things in a box under her bed that she rarely opened. She missed her garden, her spacious house but, I think, she grieved only over my grandfather's insatiable appetite for other women.

In Hungary, Transylvania is called Erdély.

It's where my grandfather's people were born.

It's where the Carpathian mountain range arcs westward, protecting the plains that were the earliest home of the Hun and later the Magyar tribes. "They were horsemen," Vili told me, "tall, fine-featured, their clothes made of spun wool and softened leather, their weapons cased in silver and inlaid with pearls. They wore beaten gold bracelets, rings on their fingers, necklaces adorned with rubies. Their horses' necks were decorated with precious stones, gold fibulae on the saddles. They so loved their horses, they were usually buried with them."

("Somebody killed the horses when the people died?"

"They didn't want to live anyway once their masters were buried."

"Oh.")

"They crossed the mountains under the cover of night, over steep, treacherous passes, carrying all their goods on their backs – they never had more than they could carry – fleeing from the Bulgars, or the Avars, or the Pechenegs, or perhaps all three. They settled in a lush, wooded land they called Erdély. With the mountains behind them they felt protected from their enemies."

I first heard about Attila the Hun from Vili. We were hanging over the balcony of our apartment trying out my new bow and arrow, which Vili had found in an old curiosity shop in the Obuda section of the city. He said the bow was made of the finest spruce, shaped like an eagle, dipped in red dye with a leather handle and sinew string, just like the ones Attila used when he laid waste to the Roman Empire. Laid waste, Vili said, meant he destroyed it. "It was an old empire, bloody, corrupt and bloated with the blood of its victims. All empires reach that stage, even this one." When Vili said "this one," I knew he meant the Soviet empire and that we were part of it. Only Hungarians, he said, would name their sons Attila.

Stories of the great plains and river valleys the Huns had found were told by their story-tellers who travelled throughout the nations, talking about the exploits of the brave and the demise of the mighty, the wisdom of those who learn to listen to the advice of the elders, and those who carry magic in their pockets and sometimes in their souls.

("What kind of magic?" "The kind that keeps you out of trouble.")

When the Magyars, who were still fighting the Pechenegs, Avars and everybody else somewhere in deepest Asia, heard of the beautiful lands their cousins, the Huns, had found, they grabbed their children and animals and followed over the same passes.

There were seven tribes with seven chiefs, said Vili. Rather than fight over who was going to be leader, the seven elected one superchief. His name was Árpád. He was the strongest, and wisest. His thick leather vest repulsed the arrows of his enemies, and he wore leather britches and deerhide boots that rarely touched the ground because he spent most of his life on his stallion. Vili promised to take me to Heroes' Square to visit him one day.

The chiefs assembled under a deer-pelt tent, and invited their people to witness a ceremony of blood that would unite them forever. Each chief, in turn, slit his forearm with a jewel-inlaid dagger, and let his blood drip into an earthenware cup. When it was almost full, the shaman, known as the taltos, mixed it with red wine, poured some onto the ground to appease the spirits of the earth, then handed it to each chief, in turn, while uttering secrets in a language no one understood, but that they all knew was more ancient even than the Magyars'. One by one, they drank from the cup. When it was empty, the taltos declared they were now united in blood and would act as one nation, not as seven separate tribes.

Vili now turned back to the arrows. They were gold-painted with black and white feathers at one end. He had tied a string to the feathery end, so we wouldn't lose them. We could shoot them over the side or up into the air so they would fall back onto the balcony. The trick was to get out of their way when they came back.

"There is an old tale about the first Hungarians," Vili said. "Do you want to hear it?"

"Does it have something to do with arrows?"

"Old tales about Hungarians always have something to do with arrows."

It was a tale about the two handsome sons of King Menrot, Hunor and Magyar, who go hunting for deer in their forests between the rivers Volga and Don, just to the West of the Ural Mountains. Being both handsome and clever, they are successful in their endeavours. Their arrows hit straight into the hearts of their prey. One would not expect less of them – at least not in this tale. As they turn for home with the fresh meat tied to their horses, they catch sight of a fabulous pair of antlers, a stag bigger and statelier than those they've already killed. Being the best of their kingdom, these two princes have no choice but to add this stag to their trophy collection. They chase it over land and water, night and day, over marshes, and forests so thick their horses must slow to a walk, through the domains of the black bear, the wild boar, even the stealthy tiger, and past the shores of the Black Sea, over steep passes and rocky ravines. Sometimes they lose sight of the prey.

The stag reappears as if to mock them, but they must go on because, being sons of King Menrot, they will not be mocked. They are determined to nail its antlers to their castle wall. Ignoring their evil intent, the stag leads them into a land so mild and lovely, they forget their original plan, lay down their bows and arrows, and begin to enjoy themselves.

The sun is warm, their horses are getting fat eating all the green grass, the brook water is sweet. To make matters perfect, they come upon a party of young girls disporting themselves with a gaggle of fairies. It was thought in those days that young girls could turn themselves into fairies if they were not grabbed first by men. No chance of that for these young sprites. Hunor and Magyar take themselves a couple of brides, and settle in this beautiful place.

No further mention of the miraculous stag, though the tale makes it clear that my ancestors would never have found Erdély had it not been for his leadership.

Most Hungarians still think of this land as their own, despite the fact that it is now part of Romania.

When I think of it as Erdély, it is a deceptively pastoral place with straw-roofed houses, and warlike people, the birthplace of heroes like János Hunyadi who beat back Sultan Mohammed's armies from the gates of Europe, and whose castle is in Erdély. At noon, when church bells ring throughout Europe, it is to celebrate his victory over the "infidel."

When I was very young I thought Kula was in Erdély because it made sense for my grandfather's people to have lived in the same place for all those hundreds of years. But it isn't. It's several hundred kilometres southwest, in Bácska, and it was a baffling accident of fate that landed Vili's grandmother so far from where she was born.

KARL SANDOR

The Man from Portugal

"Yes, I am coming for a glass of wine. Give it another five minutes, the traffic is lighter around nine," he says, waits until the sharp click disconnects his line, then puts the receiver back onto its cradle. The car key is on the table in the kitchen. Like a conductor who cues the orchestra behind his back he moves his right hand, in a soft, round motion, touching the edge of his wallet in the right hip pocket. He would enjoy the twenty-minute drive. He takes the key from the door, steps outside and locks it. The grey paint on the wooden steps leading to the narrow concrete walk-way seems wet in the porch-light overhead. The latch is loose on the garage door; he needs both hands to close it when inside. He walks by the car to avoid the long nails keeping the aluminum ladder on the wall. He pulls down on the clothes-line wire of the latch, opens the door, steps outside and closes it. A short piece of the wire hangs outside, pinched between the closed doors. The car is left behind. He is facing north. He walks towards the two garbage cans standing opposite the garage door. Four steps to the north, now he turns left. A dog stops and looks at him then sits by the fence and waits. He walks on the light uphill towards Fraser Street. On the left the house is pink at five minutes past nine on the June sixteenth. At the alley corner he steps to the right to let a green car turn. A girl of oriental origin is waiting for the bus. It will take her north, then the bus will turn west. He turns to his right and walks toward the traffic light at a distance of two city blocks. The man who walks by him avoids his eyes. If he keeps the pace of his walk the traffic light facing him will turn green when he is ready to step off the curb. The boy who walks quicker than he does passes

him on the right; the noise of the cars is stronger now, it
swallows the sound of the boy's denim pant legs rubbing
each other. His jeans are too big for him. The light is green.
He steps off the curb and walks twenty-five steps straight
north, now he turns left, to the west. The light is green, the
street is running downhill now. Under the roof of the bus
stop a lady is wearing heavy sweaters, she has slow circulation. The bus is not coming yet. His steps are an inch longer
now. He avoids a child who steps in front of him. There are
three others waiting for the bus. The light at the corner
makes the lower part of the faces visible. For a while all will
travel west on Broadway. After three blocks he must turn
right, north, to Main Street. A bus comes, no one looks at
him from its windows. The child who twisted her hands free
from the hand of her mother is not visible. She must be on
the other side of the bus, talking to a man from Portugal. He
is embarrassed, his hands are dirty; he is a roofer working
for a company in Victoria. The man who owns the company
lives in Victoria. The name of his mother is Victoria. Once
she told her son that he should not bother with the trade that
was dear to Uncle Martin.

The man is tired. He looks at his hands. The mother
looks at her magazine, the child is talking to the man. The
man does not understand the words of the child. The part of
the magazine that the mother is interested in is missing; she
drops the magazine onto the floor. The child turns away
from the man. The driver corrects the run of his vehicle, now
it parallels the curve of the street. This is only possible if they
are on the bus, they could be, but perhaps the child and the
mother took the other that followed the first. The name of
the father of the first bus-driver is Martin. The name of the
bus-driver's dog is Martin. The bus driver has roses by the
garage wall and he is not sure what the flies like, the paint
on the wall or the roses. Tomorrow if the morning turns out
to be sunny he would burn the green, the indescribably

beautiful green of the back of the fly with his magnifying glass. He would feel like a participant in magic when the dark green starts to boil. The letters of the bus are not visible. It could be that the driver who has the garden and the dog is driving the second bus. It would be good to be certain! Yes it would be good to be certain . . . yes they took the second bus, the mother is looking at him on his way to drink one or two or three glasses of wine. The child pushes his tongue out, then flat onto the glass of the window. Where is the man from Portugal? The first bus is three city blocks from him. He would not go that far. At Main he would have turned to right, to the north.

Three blocks to the west the first bus slows down. The child is not on it, but the man from Portugal could be. It is impossible to be certain about the location of the man from Portugal! The store closes at five thirty, its clock shows nineteen past nine. In its window the motorbike is black, now more black than red, then more red than black, now it is all red because of the sign overhead. The bikes are made in Germany. Tomorrow he could buy one. After nine. He knows a little about driving a motorbike. There could be an accident. With a Big Rig. He would run head on into a big rig on the summit of an uphill, but cannot decide about who would drive on the wrong side of the road. Who would drive the forty-two-thousand-pound vehicle. Would the name of the driver be Martin? That would be impossible because Martin is walking one two three four five six seven eight nine ten steps ahead of him. Martin is from Victoria. At ten he was the best student in his class. His mother was so happy! Her son would be a scientist or a prime-minister. In grade eleven he won a competition organized by the National Society of Mathematicians. The same year he claimed inter-national recognition with his essay on the Boyai-Lo-bachevskii theorem. Martin walks nine steps in front of him.

In grade twelve Martin told his mother that he wanted to be a roofer like Uncle Martin.

Uncle Martin does not like him because the grade-twelve student Martin has puffy cheeks and roofers do not. He went back to school to graduate. He was the master of his subjects, but not of the saliva that accumulated at the dam of his lower lip every time when he was lost in thought. One two three four five six seven seven, Martin is eight steps in front of him. His teachers disliked him. If Martin is walking eight steps ahead, who is driving the big rig? Who is driving the big rig with the speed that will make it appear at the summit of the uphill at the exact moment of the appearance of the black bike? At that exact moment he would walk beside the man who is seven steps ahead. Is the name of the driver Martin? Death is guaranteed. The driver will not come to the funeral. Martin received a scholarship in spite of the dislike of his teachers. Even his mother lost her patience when she heard the noise of the slow whistle of the bubbling saliva. The man is six steps ahead. Hurry now! Martin is happy but not because the government gave him the money, he is happy because Uncle Martin in Victoria agreed to employ him on roofs not higher than two storeys, starting school holiday.

The man who is walking ahead of him is in his early forties. He is five steps ahead. Because of his posture, that is the reason for the estimate of forty-two years. There is a book under his arm, now in between his fingers. Right hand. His head is slightly tilted to the right. He does not know that he is being followed. It is very hard to satisfy mother. She talks with such conviction. She doesn't like the mail service and pure research. Sends him for soda water at five to eleven. The store is closed. At home, on an unused Christmas card he declines the invitation of the National Research Council. He drops the card into a mail box on his way to work. This is a repair job says Uncle Martin. In the course of securing

the first load of tar to the rope around the chimney Uncle
Martin loses his balance and falls onto the pavement. He is
dead. Mother is crying. Young Martin decides to take over
the business and comes over to investigate an offer of partnership that would enable the firm to expand. Mother likes
the idea of partnership and does not say anything about
young Martin's desire to ride the bike made in Germany.
There are two small blue moles under the left nipple of the
man who turns ahead towards the window of a record store.
He notices a man, two steps behind, imagining a story of the
life of the man who is walking in front of him. Even with him
now, even with him now, should ask him now: what is your
name, or that's not good, should ask him: is your name
Martin? Because if your name is not Martin then Martin is
the driver of the big rig, driving in the wrong lane, he is
coming finally! The man on his left walks perceptibly slower
now, with one swift move he should reach over and open the
shirt to see if he has a mole or not. In the dark he would have
to bend close, the size of the moles were not imagined, it
could be that they were small, what if his name is Martin and
he has two moles under his left nipple? What if the man is a
roofer from Victoria? His name could be Jack! He turns to
the man on his left. The two faces are close to each other.
He asks – Is your name Martin?

   The man looks at the book in his hand as if he did not
hear the question then steps off the sidewalk. His name
could be Jack. Then let Martin drive the big rig! He lives
with his mother in Victoria. Her name is Victoria. He fails
eleventh grade. Uncle Martin hires him, but is disgusted by
the way the boy is sucking back saliva from the dam of his
lower lip when he cannot find an answer to a question. Jack
is gone. A bus has stopped after crossing Martin. The people
are stepping off the bus then walk into the wall of the house
or into the doorway of the restaurant. Two of the passengers

are agitated. There is no time to imagine the cause of their excitement. He turns right onto Main Street.

In the alley, thirty-six feet to his right, occupying three quarters of the width of the driveway stands a truck. Its driver left the lights on. The letters are not visible on the door. The motor is not running. The trailer is for refrigerated goods. He cannot see the driver. When he walks into the beams of the headlights he feels transparent. He looks for the driver without slowing his walk. It is downhill now until the hotel where the viaduct starts. He turns west and when the light changes to green he crosses the street. On the narrow walkway of the viaduct he feels abandoned. In the case of an attack there would be no way to avoid confrontation. The walkway is forty-two inches wide. Below, on the left, men and women are coming out from the bus depot or from the post office or from the theatre or from the square where the trees could cancel groups of people. There are no children with them. Children must have enough rest for tomorrow. Most of the children will go to school tomorrow. They must learn so they will understand when they are grown men and women. Children should not be left home for their nightmares. The day after the day after tomorrow they don't have to go to school, it will be Saturday then Sunday, Oh but not all children will live that long! The mommies and daddies don't know which of the children will not have tomorrow.

The third floor button is not shiny like the first and the second. Mother said that it is good to live on the third floor. The birds live high over the ground. It would be very good to go with her. She goes at fifteen minutes to eight to get to Grandmother at the bus-depot, then they walk across the square to the theatre. Grandmother never stays, she goes back with the last bus to Victoria. Perhaps she wins something when she comes to the theatre? They keep the prize for themselves. Mother never says anything about winning, but

Mister Sylvester does. He says that the one who first reaches the horizontal bar when climbing the rope will win the Good Progress Award of all the first graders. No one in the class could beat him if the climb were on the curtains, he would get the award, would win even if his name is Martin and not Victoria. Climb then tear it quickly so it won't move behind the radiator as if Arthur from the Hollandish restaurant had climbed into the room from the fire escape. His Emma wants to have a kid for dinner. Emma loves to eat kids. Emma has much brown wavy hair and smiles as she asks the child – would you like a toy train? She has her own teeth, and pats and strokes the child harder than another woman would: to feel the packing of meat around the neck. The window is facing south. On Thursdays Mother uses words that start with the letter d: dear, delight, despair then dreadful. What would she say, dear or dreadful, when she had to look at the body? It must be Arthur. Emma is hungry! He takes his pillow, pulling the blanket behind, he hops onto the window – Mister Sylvester should see him now – he grabs the curtain and pulls on it, the rods let go, he jumps. The house that Grandmother sold in Lethbridge had a fire escape under the bedroom window. It was painted white. He falls onto the sidewalk. The blanket lands on the wires of the trolley.

In the three storey-high apartment all the windows are dark. It could be a store-house. Then little Martin would not be waiting for his mother.

The art gallery is dark, quite like a cemetery. A young tree planted into the sidewalk has an unusually large crown of leaves. The small rivers of light that filter through the branches remind him of wet streaks in the fur of a cat. In the tunnel that leads the pedestrians up on to the sidewalk by the causeway crossing the park, the light bulb now belongs to the collection of the bulk standing on a wooden box. She wears a fur coat and the glass cover of the light is still in her hand. Perhaps she needed the light bulb. Her left hand is still in the cavity of the concrete wall where the wires are waiting. She could get electrocuted. She would drop the light bulb into the sea when going to Victoria. He walks by her. The underpass leads to a bus terminal on the left, to the side walk by the causeway on the right. The light of the oncoming cars are building. He discovers a rhythm in the occurrence of the passing cars and now the noise of the cars is bearable. The sky is black-blue. The bridge is visible now. There is a clear pattern inside the seemingly indecipherable messages of the imaginable directions; inside the Norths and Wests, Martins are waiting for mother Victoria; perhaps the driver of the big rig is the man from Portugal. One would never never be sure. The ground vibrates under his feet because of the difference between the density of the bridge and that of the understructure of the road leading to the bridge, or because of the cars? Or because of the wind or because of the earth tremor? Or because he imagines that the ground vibrates when it does not? The bridge leads toward north. Not being able to find an answer to the question about the cause of the vibration of the road makes him impatient. At the centre of the bridge he stops and lifts his left leg over the rectangular bar of the handrail, then securing a safe hold lowers his body on the outside of the rail. He finds a comfortable stand for his left then his right foot between the balusters. His palms are dry. The trail is cold. He is on his way for a glass or two or three of wine. He left the car home. The wine is waiting. He lets his body move away from the rail then he pulls his body back close to the rail. He smiles. He does not have to think of Martins or brown haired Emma. Does not have to know where North or West is. How did the blanket get over the trolley wires? Now he lets go with both hands, he tilts backward, grabs the rail with his left hand. The left is weaker than the right. When the body is moving backward one is free of the delirium of insatiable imagination, now he is not excited by the directions of the roads. The wine is waiting, but perhaps the man from Portugal . . . ? With all his strength he arches into the dive. With a clear mind he tumbles into the delicious miasma, toward certainty, mesmerized by the miracle of his unexpected liberty.

ÉVA SÁRVÁRI

During Office Hours

"Hello?"

"Is that Mrs. Madarász?"

"Yes. What can I do for you?" (She has a pleasant, low voice.)

"We don't know one another. My brother asked me to call you. I have a message for your husband. Jancsi can't go for his piano lesson this evening. He had to go to Hamilton on business and won't be back till late tonight, so he couldn't call himself. But he's very sorry the lesson has to be postponed, and asked me to . . ."

"Oh, you are very kind, thank you. It's good you called. You see, my husband has so much to do anyway. He hardly has any free time, and would so much like to work on his newest composition, the A-minor concerto . . ."

(I try to say good-bye.)

"Well, I'm sorry I disturbed you . . ."

"That's all right. I have a few minutes free. (I don't, but she doesn't ask about that.) I just got home from the Dominion – prices are terrible! Only yesterday I was saying to my husband how much everything's gone up just in the year we've been in Canada. But I don't want to bother the poor man with my domestics . . ."

(It looks like she wants to feed her troubles to me instead.) "Yes, there's inflation all over the world, Mrs. Madarász."

"And yet we shouldn't say a thing here in Canada. It's still the best here. How much worse it was in Germany, and even there it was better than in Hungary! But my husband wanted to leave Germany at all costs. I didn't want to, and we had a few lively arguments about it, till I thought, let him have his way, after all he's the head of the family, isn't that right? (It is, but who's interested?) But no, I don't want to complain, because financially it is better here in Canada. And now that he's got his appointment to be a high school music teacher he'll make good money and our life will be a lot easier. We don't have many debts, but we had to buy a piano – that's necessary for his teaching – and if you're going to buy one, there's no sense getting a piece of junk . . . But we only bought the piano, the car and the living room furniture on credit, and now – thank God – the payments will be easy to make."

"Well, I'm glad things are better, Mrs. Madarász. (I can't slam down the receiver, much as I would like to. My boss might come back any minute and he doesn't like it if I make private calls during office hours.) I'm glad that you're happy in Canada."

"By now, thank God, yes. But the start was very hard. Students came slowly; for a while there at the beginning he didn't have a single one . . . You know how it is, a strange name in a strange city. As for me, I would have taken any kind of job, but I couldn't find work. I'm not young any more, and unfortunately I cannot speak a word of English. I don't know why, since I speak four languages fluently (fluent Hungarian, no doubt about it!), and I am still incapable of learning English, absolutely incapable! So I could only work in a Hungarian place, but where can you find one? Who could I turn to? I tried often enough, but it's not so simple. I applied as a salesclerk at one of the Hungarian fashion stores and the owner said over the phone 'We need someone young.' I told him I was forty-nine."

"Well, it's true we live in a cruel world, Mrs. Madarász. It's not easy to find work. The statistics show there's never been so much unemployment in Canada before." (I wonder what does she look like, this woman?)

"But finally there was an opening for cleaning offices . . . and I, the daughter of a world renowned surgeon, with a high-school diploma! But then, there's no shame in work, is there? I took the job, too, except I got sick. We were hardly in Toronto four or five years and I wound up in hospital."

(Now that she's told me this, politeness demands, after all, that I say a few kind words.) "I hope you have fully recovered since . . ."

"The thing is, I haven't. I have dizzy spells and head-aches, and a buzzing in my ears all the time. But this isn't an after-effect of the operation, it's something else. I came around perfectly well after the surgery, although it was serious. They took out both my ovaries."

(If this woman starts telling me all her forty-nine years' worth of illness my boss is going to come back and kick me out on the spot.)

"My only fortune is that the good Lord blessed me with such a fine husband and such a good, well-mannered boy as my son. He's not like these Canadian hippies. Oh, the proper European upbringing shows, doesn't it. And the close family life. The only thing that bothers me is that we had to interrupt his schooling for a year, partly because of language difficulties, but that alone would have been all right, the young can always pick up a language here or there easily enough. I'll tell you the truth: it was mostly for financial reasons. Unfortunately, we have a great need for money. István's working in a Becker's store now, but next year he'll go back to school. I hope they'll take him in the twelfth grade. The blessed good boy brings every penny home. Tell me, dear, have you seen the like these days in this rotten, callous world, when young people have it so good they don't know what to do with themselves?"

(My ear's gone totally numb from the receiver.) "Yes, you're certainly a fortunate woman to have such a good son. And I'm glad that in the end everything's turned out well for you here in Toronto. And now if you'll excuse me . . ."

"Yes, maybe now I can say that in the end everything turned out well, it's just that in the beginning things went wrong. Do you know what was the worst of all? That we were so lonely here. Not a relative, not a friend. My husband had a younger cousin at first, but he got transferred to Montreal and we were left to ourselves. What good's a telephone when it never rings? That's the only reason I'm sorry we didn't stay in Freiburg. We left a lot of good friends there. I guess it's easier for my husband; you know how men are . . . they just pick up their hats and go . . . And then, he's got his students. But I'm just left by myself, day after day. If I could have someone here, not even my best friend Elli, just someone, anyone, at least now and then . . . If I could at least talk to someone on the phone; if only you knew how good it is to talk to you now, and I don't even know you."

"Certainly, mankind is a social being. No man's an island." (No! that wasn't right, to talk to her in generalities. She deserves one or two warm, friendly words.)

"And if you're alone you begin to imagine things. I don't know if you've ever been that way. I've never told this to anyone, dear, but at one time I imagined that my husband . . . Well, why beat around the bush. Now I know that it wasn't just my imagination. It's true that he is not an outwardly attractive man – a thin, frail creature – but how he knows the way to a woman's heart! It's not that he's not good to me – the opposite. My dear little one – even now he calls me, after twenty-six years of marriage – my dear little one . . . I still don't know how it happens, but there's always

one among his students; they look into each other's eyes
. . . But I know what men are like – why should my husband
be different?

(She continues haltingly between sobs, while I'm struck
dumb and wide-eyed. My boss is standing in front of my
desk, watching me coldly for who knows how long.)

"We're both grown up, and women, and no one else is
listening anyway. I know how important the married life is
for a man, and if a wife can't offer the things in that sphere
for a while . . . But maybe that wasn't even the problem with
my husband, maybe it's just that he's such a foolish romantic
. . . He finds someone who's younger and prettier than I,
then he's finished . . . He falls into it as though he were
twenty. Right now, one of his students – I can't deny she's a
pretty woman, and light blonde hair always was a weakness
of his. And if a blonde, slender thing like this looks up at him
as though he were a demigod – which is no wonder, since
my husband is indeed very big in the music world, you'll see,
his name will be remembered . . . But he swoons. And I, who
am just a wife, nothing else, swallow hard and don't say a
thing . . . I act as though I hadn't noticed anything . . . Only
a few know how much I suffer . . ."

"If only I could console you somehow, Mrs. Madarász . . ." (My words stumble too. The slightest excuse and
I'd burst into tears. The boss meanwhile has gone into his
office, but I know this doesn't mean the storm clouds have
gone. It doesn't matter, I'll get myself another job! I'm still
young and I speak English well.)

"But then I always think, if he didn't love me, he
wouldn't stay with me. And he's such a good man, even his
presence soothes me . . . Of course he gets excited when he
finds a good pianist among all those tin-eared students, and
he can't help it if the pianist happens to be a young blonde
. . . The kiss on the hand I happened to see the other day

doesn't amount to love, even if both of them did blush . . .
and there was nothing like that in the letter I found in his
coat pocket . . . Maybe he didn't even want to keep it a
secret, but just forgot to show it to me . . . And such a pretty
young woman must have ten men wrapped around each
finger – why would she cast her eyes right at my husband?
And why should I ask him to account for every minute of the
day? After all, he needs his solitude once in a while, so he can
be alone with his thoughts, since he's a creative artist . . . Isn't
that true? Maybe I bore him sometimes with my chatter . . .
I know little about music, and I'm a terrible pianist. Maybe
I don't offer my husband what I should, but then who ever
finds a perfect life's-companion in his life's companion?"

(I manage to conceal the fact that my tears are flowing,
and answer in my casual voice.) "You're a very brave woman,
Mrs. Madarász . . ."

"You see, dear, I told you just now that I don't have a
friend, but all the same I always find someone who shakes
me out of the hopelessness, who pours life back into me . . .
Even now, it felt wonderful that you so kindly consoled me
. . . I certainly thank you. And you know, the Lord always
helps me through all kinds of cares and woes . . . But now I
have to say good bye, I hope you won't mind. Jesus Mary!
My son will be home any minute – he comes home for lunch
every day and I haven't got a thing ready yet . . . Don't mind
me, but I have to go. God bless you. I'll pass your message
on to my husband. Thank you for calling."

"Good bye, all the best . . . (how stupid that sounds. I
should have said something more meaningful.)

And I can't help it, I can't keep back my tears as I stand
in front of my boss's desk and hand him the result of my
morning's work: a short letter, barely half a page of typing –
and in my choked voice I say to him:

"Mr. Flemming, don't be angry with me, please. I'll

never, never make another private call from the office during working hours. I promise."

Translated by Karl Sandor and George Payerle

JOSEPH SERES

What News?

In no way
can I tell you anything new,
for well you know this:
winter lingers still,
the snow traces hard blotches
on the geometry of rooftops
and black houses hold
thawing kisses
in eternal Spring.

In no way
can I tell you anything new,
for surely you have intimations
of what's beautiful, what surpasses us;
stars in the sky's blue meadow.
Moon in the cold lake trembles
when human desire gleams
vainglorious, understandably
in your eyes.

In no way
can I tell you anything new,
for truly you must feel
what's good –
what calms you,
what excites you,
what thrives and what decays –

but what you understand
you don't often feel;
feel it now
and say: this is wonderful.

Translated by George Payerle

You Do Well

You can fall on your knees
before the god dreamed in your imagination's light
and I'll say:
you do well then.
You enact
what excites your blood
your true self
in success, in failure,
in crisis and in conflict.
Don't turn back.
Go on just like this!

You can dream what is unimaginable in logic,
because it is the way you can get done
what's impossible to get done today
and I'll say:
you do well then.
You act
as your heart beats
and you can be content:
no one does it better,
because having an eye to the start and the finish
means more than bending a knee
to received truth and expounded theory.

Your own light can blaze up in you,
if you tend it and not another's lamp
that glows in your private cosmos.
I'll say this:
you do well then,
because your thought ignites, wicklike, with truth;
because there lies the lake, where its waters lap
and from a tossed stone its bright ring appears.

Translated by George Payerle

ÁGNES SIMÁNDI

Golden Cupolas
(Andrei Rublew's Revolt)

sometimes from the depth of my body
wild dreams erupt like rivulets and I tremble
in fear of the hours that keep me apart from you

this is not the revolt I have longed for
the cold arrogance of the troops passing through
the agony of the desiccated lice,
the ticking, as the angels buried in sticking glue and lime
strip their wings from the past because only what exists
can be poured into a mold but to utter the word
to ring the bell is allowed only in the room inhabited
by people they'll come forward unbolt the door
because they want to come closer everything else is like
a dream, its own a shapeless statue, a drift, a keyless
torment: the denial of death all this time all
I cared about was the golden cupolas
here the ablution has deepened into ceremony and
the symbol of the pure hand and heart stirs up the lake
of intellect, in tumult the mind's eye tumbles faces and
      words:
the disciples of Basileus hide their soft-voiced prayers
in their solitude, incandescent in veneration I liked
to go on pilgrimage to their springs,
to the nests, nursing me to my humanity, they beckoned
me all the time this is not the revolt I have longed for
cutting across the pores of my being maybe I came
to life so that you, while coming upon my secrets,
should stumble into the failure of approaching because

the tearing gaze of a talent will always look out for its
own kind don't fear, even in the hearts that now trip
me up the solitude speaking through my colours
will remain a wound that is irrevocable, that can never
      heal this I believe. I know.

Translated by Erika Simon

Toronto

Not to stop halfway
not to look back. This is
what the moment bequeathed me

I was embraced by pain,
gently stirring,
while the slow measure
of leave taking

carried the little family
– your life – to faraway
zones of safety, shelter.

who knows whether the grass
of the pastures in Egypt
is richer

whether solitude
weaves there a stronger
belt around our waist

how little does it matter.
but as long as your lips
form the words

in Hungarian

the kiss also can be only
of a certain kind

under the tropic of this
fine new city
emerging, undressed,
from its morning mask.

Translated by Erika Simon

Emmaus

the river bed is exhausted, the windswept
grass awaits to be burned in sacrifice
in the mirror a stranger's face twitches at you.
before, you looked back even twice from
the windows of departing trains, fading into
the distance, or cast the net way ahead
the quietly swinging river, and you were not
interested in footnotes, in shied remarks,
in the doors closing into your face.
like everybody else in the chaos, in this
last minute before sinking, you lived
in the calm that whatever will be, will be.
it is not death we have to fear
only the bleakness of the last moments
and the gangrened vestiges of memory. Somehow
it must have been this great simplicity
that drove them all into that electrically charged
atmosphere that precedes explosion,
the betrayal of the objects, the loneliness
frozen to the hotel stairs, the solitary spasm

of that guy the other day who looked
to the subway tracks to find his peace.
I have not seen him, only his body covered
by blanket; it was pushed ahead by troops
of running firefighters. The colour of death
is orange I thought then and felt a thirst
for the air suddenly escaping from that narrow
underground corridor. But then the fact that
one feels exhausted does not mean that s/he is
ripe enough to leave here I heard the words
within, as if someone were heading, once more,
toward Emmaus and the dust got between
my toes while we debated the Word letter
by letter we were in search of the forefathers
sinuous snake-headed literary sources,
someone even leafed through our volume
of Denzinger, this here he said, is the most
beautiful, this irrevocable fact we can
definitely not call a symbol, this something
that we cannot relate to literary source,
this something for which you would all
give away everything, they could slice off
the flesh from your bones or even boil it
in oil on a blood-soaked feast but you
would let it happen, because the body
does not count, beloved, it is only appearance,
you would give away everything, you,
who are seemingly happier then the rest,
the vast masses of creatures also there
should be someone ready for sacrifice
after all, he went on – but his hands
paused above the table,
to divide among us the piece of bread.

Translated by Erika Simon

GABRIEL SZOHNER

The First Woman

From his window all he could see was the illuminated giant red clock on top of the C.N.R. railway station. It was 2:00 A.M. Leaning his head against the cool wall, lying in his bed staring at the two arms of the clock chasing each other frightfully fast like mad beasts running a wild race against his nerves, disjoining his thoughts.

More than three years had passed since his arrival to Canada and for more than three years the blazing clock was the focal point in his landscape. He stared at it days and nights, witnessing the weeks, months, dragged by their two arms from one number to the next slowly, mercilessly, around and around. He stared at the clock when he just day-dreamed, fantasizing about his paintings which would one day be exhibited in the world's best galleries, when he imagined intelligent people being his friends, enjoying fame when it did not matter if one had rusty red hair, small yellow eyes, worn concrete-like skin, a pathetically fragile, deformed body. The clock was there, laughing at him, ridiculing him, whispering to him, "You are what you are in your own space, on the merry-go-round of my time. From sunrise to sunset from sunset to sunrise. Trapped, crucified to these numbers."

But this night he was not dreaming. This night the clock, betraying the past, itself and him rushed its arms on the circular track, totally outracing him. This night there was a girl beside him. The first woman ever to share his food, his bed.

A few hours earlier, with one final revenge he had smashed his canvas and paint brush against the kitchen wall, and kicking the worn chair into the corner he burst out to the rainy street.

He wanted to soak to the bone, catch pneumonia, get hit by a drunk driver, fall into a workman's hole and break both arms so he could never hold a paint brush again. He yearned for something fatal to happen he ran with closed eyes across the street, then walked slowly around and around a single block. He wept, then desperately tried to look up against the beating rain without blinking an eyelid. His shirt open, soaked to his trembling skinny body. He wanted thunder, blazing sky, lightning from hell, but there was only the pale green neon sign above the door of the Bank of Commerce dancing a slow primitive dance on his shoulders, humming a melancholy tune on his wet white skin. Never had he wanted to feel so sorry for himself as he did now. Facing him, in the huge glass door, a clown, staring back at him, dressed in the faded hand-out colours of the night street.

He remembered that he had thirty-two dollars and seventy-two cents in that bank and that was it. The few paintings that were accepted by the town's smallest gallery laid against the wall in the storage room. They did not ask him outright to remove them but surely it would not be long. Thirty two-dollars and seventy-two cents.

"So what the heck would you do?" he shouted at the clown. "Join the nine-to-five slaves, labour your soul, your conscience away. Thinking about nothing in this whole rotten world but how long your job would last, what would the next job be. Or join the decayed line of the welfare collectors or . . . or this. Pounding out hard decisions over every damn penny. If they should be spent on a can of beans or a tube of paint, a mouthful of meat or a brush."

The clown had no solution to offer. Shrugging off Franz's attack he shouted every insult back. "The hell with you," muttered Franz. "You're not even a friend. If you want to know, a friend has to be either above or below you, so you just feel sorry for yourself and I'll do the same." He turned heading straight down the street.

At this time of night there wasn't a soul walking on the street and despite the rushing traffic, despite the neon lights, he felt deserted. The cars became slimy insects. And as a defeated rebel who was just about to lose the last days of his freedom, he stuck his hands into the pockets of his trousers, he walked on aimlessly. He reached the end of Main Street, four or five blocks away skid road began. At times he walked over there to find some alcoholic to talk to. At least they tended to listen. Tonight he didn't want to see any of them. He wanted to be alone. The sight of broken down buildings, junkyards, crummy second-hand stores, sick old warehouses created a painful awareness. Suddenly a hand reached out to him and a face came so close that he stopped promptly to avoid collision.

"Can you spare some change?"

A girl stood in front of him, wearing an old leather jacket, blue jeans, her hair soaked tight to her scalp.

Franz searched in his pockets. He knew he didn't have a penny on him, but he felt a refusal, a simple no, even if true, would sound cruel. "I'm sorry," he muttered. "Uh . . . Where are you going? Perhaps I can help you. Help you some other way."

"Forget it," said the girl firmly and turned away.

"Where are you going?" Franz asked again. "It's sure miserable out here. Could I walk you home?"

"I've no home."

"I haven't got a penny, believe me."

"Don't apologize." She stepped back, as if this was all she wanted to accomplish, nothing mattered now, like a child hiding behind a chair.

"I live only six blocks away. Couldn't stand the smell of paint any longer . . . I can make you a cup of tea. At least you could dry off, get warmed." The girl turned to face him. "And what after?"

"After what? What do you mean?"

"Yeah, after your cosy tea?"

"Oh, don't misunderstand me," smiled Franz. "You can trust me. I'm not the type. I wasn't thinking of anything like that."

"You got some kind of an accent," the girl stated.

"Yes, I'm German."

She looked away, "I don't like immigrants. Don't trust them. You know Tony?"

"No."

"Everybody knows Tony. He's an immigrant. He thinks he's a smart ass. Fancy clothes, penthouse and all that. A sonofabitch." She nodded in self agreement.

"I don't know him. Never heard of him. Is he that bad?"

"He's a pig. But why should it bother you?"

"Perhaps it shouldn't" said Franz, ready to walk away. But he looked at the girl once more. In spite of her strong words, she looked so helpless. What could he tell her to cheer her up? They stood there for a moment. She looked left and right, avoiding Franz's penetrating glance. Finally he spoke, "You sure you don't want me to accompany you? It's getting late at night. I can walk you downtown. There are more people around. Easier to find help."

"I know how to get there."

"Sorry. I thought you were from out of town."

She smirked looking down Main Street, her face tensed as if she was wanting to remember or just remembered something she didn't want to.

"Let's go for that tea," she said still glancing down the street. But she said the words so simply that this abrupt change crumbled the pitying emotion building up in Franz. "I live only six blocks from here," repeated the boy and offered her his arm. She refused to take it.

"Let's run before we melt," he suggested.

"I'm too goddamn stiff to run," the girl said. "Couldn't get more soaked anyway." She walked a step behind him, looking straight ahead, letting her arms dangle freely.

Opening the door to his apartment he apologized. "It's a horrible smell in here, never failed to boil up the acid in my stomach. I do my painting in the kitchen."

"You some kind of an artist?"

"Oh, just a fake. You might say I am just pretending to be one. Only fooling myself."

"What are you talking about?"

"Take your coat off if you like. I'll make us some hot tea. By the way, my name is Franz."

The girl glanced through the paintings that hung around the walls, then fixed her eyes on the radiator under the window. "Does that thing work?" She stepped towards the window.

"Yes. You can put your coat on it to dry."

In the kitchen he made tea, toast, found cheese and sausage in the fridge. The girl sat on the radiator, staring down at the floor. Franz looked at her, offering her the plate. "Not much, but it should hit the spot. What are you contemplating?"

"I'm not contemplating anything. I'm just warming my bum."

"You thinking of Tony?"

"Tony who?"

Franz handed her the tea. "Sometimes I drink it with rum. Want some? Warms you up faster."

"Wanna get me drunk?" She looked around in search of the bottle. "I'm used to the booze. I can drink like a fish. What's one more alcoholic."

Franz poured some rum in both cups. "I have to admit," she said, "they're more charismatic, aren't they? I mean they're different than what you grow up with around here. All the European men are charismatic. I don't know how to explain it. Tony sure was. He gave me speed the other day. It sure beats liquor."

"I've never tried any of that stuff," Franz said smiling. "I'm a sissy."

"They're good. Like orgasm, a thousand times over."

"Aren't you worried?"

"Why should I be? Who cares?"

"What if you get hooked?"

"Jesus, you're something else! You sure you live around here? I hope you don't think I'm too rotten. That's what he kept telling me. Spitting bullshit before you know the person. My parents were honest about me."

"I am sorry. Do your folks live in Vancouver?"

"They do alright."

"What happened? How come you're on your own?"

"They gave me the old boot. Any more questions?"

"Sorry," said Franz, shaking his head.

"Must you apologize all the time? Don't think they liked me to begin with. I sure as hell didn't like them. I don't remember ever wanting them around."

"That's hard to believe. I mean, it's hard to understand that a daughter . . . How about some more tea?"

"He was older, more sophisticated, a big shot, you

know. Made me proud the way he cared about me. At first, that is. But I took off."

"Why did you leave him?"

Her face became troubled as if the time had come for her to stand up against some injustice. "He was a pig, that's why . . . bringing all those monkeys home, hairy no good foreigners, guys who couldn't piss straight into a toilet bowl, speaking some dumb language, playing cards, showing off their muscles like a bunch of freaks. Then he came straight out telling me what he had in mind. Wanting me to have sex with them all. What hurt the most was when I found out that he charged them for it.

Franz looked at her bewildered. "How old are you?" The girl was going to answer him methodically, but changed her mind. "Oh shit, I won't lie to you. I'm fifteen. Alright? Gonna throw me out?"

"No, I won't." Then he looked around. "But there's only one single bed."

"But you do have chairs." She looked around and noticed that one of the chairs by the window was smashed to pieces. Then pointed at the paintings. "Did you do all that? They stink, don't they?

"In more than one way."

"What are they? I mean, what are they supposed to show?"

"My soul."

She twisted the corner of her mouth. "You should take up photography instead. At least you could show something that others could understand. Where's the bed?"

"It's a chesterfield. It opens up."

"Gonna make it, then?"

Franz opened up the old chesterfield, took a sheet, a blanket, a pillow, and by the time he turned toward her, she stood there naked. "I always sleep on the right side," she said. "Do you snore? They sure could stand some washing." She pointed at the bedsheet and the cover.

Franz was too shy to look straight at her body. Afraid to show his inexperience with women, but she had a figure . . . She was no longer a child, she had a strong, rich, woman's figure, full breasts with nipples standing upward, strong curving hips, stubborn blonde curvy pubic hair, growing thick outward onto her thighs. A warm satisfaction vibrated through his body. How things have changed around him. Only a few hours ago he felt lonely, his place hostile, his spirit hopeless. Now the place felt like home. He went to the washroom, brushed his teeth, combed his hair, turned off the light and lay down beside the girl. She was fast asleep, clamp, heavy like a huge stone on the ocean floor.

He felt putting his arms around her, give her a gentle hug, or just touch her skin, to show her his sincere friend-ship. He wanted to make her realize that all he wanted was to protect her, to weave her future into his. He reached out to touch her, his white arm trembled in the blue-grey air and stopped inches away from the girl's shoulder. He wanted to hold her head between his hands, kiss her, kiss away her sadness, her stubborn rebellion, her feeling of rejection. But he also had a growing desire to make love to her.

And what if he just started doing it? Would she open up for him with a welcoming hug? Or would she push him away in contempt?

He reached out again and touched her fine blonde hair with his fingertips and whispered in kindness, "I love you, girl."

The clock implied a new beginning. It was three-forty-five, and the morning was bringing a new phase in his life. But the girl's presence had already begun to shift and slowly slip away, leaving him stranded. He put on his paint-smeared overcoat and went into the kitchen. He picked up the canvas from the floor, placed it onto the kitchen table against the wall. Then picked up the largest brush, soaked it into the turpentine, he brushed the beginning of some odd still life on the canvas into a mess. And into this muddy grey background he painted a new composition, a bed, a woman's figure surrounded by flowers.

She would have laughed at him, just like so many other people, if she wasn't so tired. He remembered, there were moments when she had a fiendish glint in her eyes; when she saw him standing by the bathroom door.

The turpentine, linseed oil and paint bit into his nostrils, his lungs. He drew only a few scrubby lines and he didn't like what he saw. After a few more tries he sat and watched the grey mess floating off the canvas, onto the kitchen table, dripping down to the floor.

"Yes," he thought, she laughed at him. Even though she wasn't a well mannered person, and she was quite inconsiderate too, that primitive innocence on her face inflamed his soul.

He turned off the light. He went back to the bedroom, sat down on the edge of the bed and tried to think of ways in which to communicate his feelings towards the girl. It was past six, he opened the window to make the air fresh when she awakens.

In the kitchen he started making breakfast, boiling eggs. He filled the kettle and put in on low heat. Then he went back, stood beside the bed and looked at the girl admiringly.

She felt the cold air, but didn't wake, just pulled her knees up tight against her belly, leaving her pale back uncovered. In the dim light it looked like marble. He tucked in the grey sheet and blanket, covering the girl gently, again touching her hair. He went to the window, looked at the clock, imagining himself with the girl back in his country, in the places of his childhood. They were holding hands while walking the gentle slopes and valleys, the green meadows and oak forests carpeted with soft moss. Wild poppies grew on the hillside, swaying their bright heads in the tender mid-summer afternoon. She was laughing, running, pulling him along. "It's so beautiful," she said in great excitement.

As she opened her eyes, almost with the same motion she sat up and threw her legs down over the side of the bed, sitting there a few seconds. Then with a sudden move she reached for her clothes on the radiator, jerking them into her lap. "At least they're dry," she muttered.

Franz watched her dress. "I was awake all night," he said. "Couldn't fall asleep. I hope it didn't bother you." The girl said nothing. "I wanted to tell you a lot of things . . ."

"Tell me what?"

"Oh, I couldn't tell you about it all just now."

"Suit yourself. Would you pass me my shoes. I hope they're dry." Franz bent down for the shoes. Handing them to her, he walked back to the window. "I know I look stupid," he whispered.

"You can't have everything, can you?"

She was all dressed. She walked to the bathroom, combed her hair with her fingers, then took a long disapproving look at the fuzzy blonde split ends. She stood there for a while, taking her hair ends, strand by strand. Finally she threw them onto her back and walked towards the door. "Thanks, huh?"

"Won't you have breakfast before you go?"

"Don't bother. They make big breakfasts every morning."

"Who?"

"Tony and the guys. Thanks again."

Franz stood with his back to the window and listened to

the wooden stairs cracking under her clunky steps. He turned and opened the window, watching her walk by on the wet pavement, rain beating down on her head, her arms dangling free. She walked slowly. At the corner she stopped, facing an empty lot scattered with debris. She stood there, staring at the broken old Chevron station sign as if waiting for it to light up.

Franz took up painting again but he couldn't stay for ten minutes in the kitchen. He had a desire to go after her, ask her to come back. The apartment was so old, so cold and empty without her. He went to the window. She was still standing at the corner, facing the oncoming traffic, her thumb in the air.

What Does the Land Dream

What does the land dream
asleep within its shapes?

trees, like still somnambulists
are unaware
of their crystal burden;
by noon, the frost
is burned away –

heavy snows fall
of their own weight

the deer starve
and the mice dance
briefly

what does the land dream
asleep within its shapes?

A Green Metal Table

we sat
near the Danube
at 3 p.m., the sun
was already red
above the west
hills

we sat
beneath
a chestnut tree
at a green, metal table

mother bought
2 pitchers of beer
and 2 cognacs

we talked
chestnuts fell

The Trapper

the trapper's shack
is a spider's home
at the edge of the spinnings

as a tin heater
thuds
thuds
in the small log room,
he sleeps naked
between furs

buried in the snow
his metal mouths
are more silent and still
than stars they exhale
a hidden death,
a breath of mink musk and honey
aniseed oil,
castors, ten-cent perfumes,

oils of decayed fish and flesh

the trapper is a trickster
making scents of entrails and essences

Walk at Midnight

the northern lights
silhouette
the rain cloud
passing
to the east

a trout jumps
thru a green reflection
mistaking stars
for fireflies upon the surface.

MIKLÓS TAMÁSI

Homesickness

If you tried to drown it in the sea,
waves would fling it at your feet.
If you hung it on a tree,
it would fall before you like fruit.

If you abandoned it in forests,
it would return as firewood for winter.
If you harried it into the clouds,
its gentle rain would touch you by summer.

If you knew how to renounce it, then
would it still be yours.
If you died without it, thus
would it outlive you.

The man hasn't lived
who can escape his shadow.
Often now you believe
it isn't there. You are the shadow.

1960

Translated by Maxim Tabory and George Payerle

August Night

The celestial earth begins to roll.
Big bear cracks his whip from the seat.
Foam tumbles, light flashes
from the spirited horses.

It's August now. That it will be autumn soon
is clear in the subtle way the cart's shape alters –
the shaft more pointed, poised for the coming
journey, far far out.

Where does it go? Past what horizons
in its endless unknown galaxy? Impossible
to count the light years.

Our narrow earth-bound journey
is not a measure of ourselves,
but oh to hitch a ride
in that great rushing cart

And break this silent barrier
this lonely walk! Here, at crossroads
it's easy to stumble
lose the way.

The brotherhood we long for
in this unchartered life
is seldom found. Perhaps that world
up there, far out in solitude
has more to give.

English version by Genevieve Bartole

EVA TIHANYI

Acrobatics

This is never easy

She watches him as he talks, memorizes
his mouth, the movements of his face
as he teeters on the tightrope of her silence,
empty seats below on either side

He feels the straight supple line
beneath his feet, tries not to think of falling

He smiles, knows his words are necessary
and that hers would only hinder his escape

From point A to point B: a simple plan,
to go from a place where she is
to a place without her

He takes step after unsteady step,
his arms outstretched for balance

All the while he is talking and talking;
his voice echoes in the spotlit darkness
as he reaches safety and descends

There is no applause
save her heartbeat in his ears,
and the knowledge that years from now
she will imagine she can remember
the exact blue of his eyes

Death Song

It will be sudden
and I will know it for a moment only

It will pierce the skin like lightning,
leap like a panther from the eyes

It will be obscene and beautiful
like graffiti on the walls of heaven

Like a willful horse, it will break rein,
order its own direction

It will seethe and it will sing
like a poet's mouth on fire

And it will wake me, it will wake me
like a stunning lash of the sun

My Grandmother's Gloves

Even her gloves revealed her: soft leather,
not a common black or ordinary brown
but a deep flamboyant orange,
the rust of late autumn, warm and supple

They are the last things I have kept,
the final detritus after all the givings-away,
the ritual removals:
buttons in plastic pill containers,
assorted remnants of cloth,
zippers, needles, thread;
her clothes all gone,

her furniture distributed

Left: these exuberant gloves
I cannot bear to part with

For when I slip my hands into them
I am held, perfectly

NANCY TOTH

thanks are given . . .

thanks are given
for selves too filled with life
for harvest: .
fruition without season.
the headed grain,
the full grape,
are threshed and pressed but once,
and you, your yield is daily
and forever
I reel and celebrate this wine.

*

the moment
before the rain,
before the poem,
is too clear.

it illumines
the tree, the grass —
the blade of grass
in the jaws of the ant.

*

let me wear the grey
as given, as orders
not always holy,
the mark and the rank
of the dying.

swaddle me
in the dark cloth
woven surely for me,
too fine for me;
give me the dark gift,
wrap me newborn
in my lovely death.

*

whose are your eyes,
and whose the stars
that lead, guide, draw me?
whose are your eyes –
they own me
by right of orbit,
by right of all
that is bound
atom to atom
since the world was made.

*

These were your kings,
and these your kingdoms
in the millenia
that give me now
my consolation.

I do not travel
to distant relics,
royal pillars of royal houses,
but marvel instead
at the palaces you build.

You proceed from pattern
weaving line after line

into line with me
until we are the pattern
that is timeless.

*

the blade of your mind
falls to the right of me,
falls to the left of me,
shines before me,
hard and clear.

I dance in lightning
on the blade of your mind,
reveling in the light touch,
reveling in the quick sound,
and the bright fire we make.

TAMÁS TUZ

With Closed Eyes

Something came nearer.
It crept through a rainbow's arc,
flattened almost to the soil.
Amidst the outcry of yellow meadows
an untimely voice was born
to try its damp wings, tender
in the azure air.

I can't remember which month it was,
April or September?
Hungrily I watched
a cloud of birds swirled up and
swooped light-winged across my fairest thoughts
under the brightness of the threatened poplars,
where my pride gleamed prismlike
as magical springs
frolicked it toward the deceitful heavens.

Lonely again,
I groom cold stiffened music
others have galloped to Marathon;
both sunspiced and moon-strained,
the wormwood-flavoured wine spills out.

Ask. I answer:
fire-birds shoot out of the marshy indifference,
a dawn-bellied panther leaps behind them;
bread and butter gild my table,
my door opens wide
to the seasonless rampant sunshine.

Do not count your diamonds,
enter my home.

English version by George Payerle

Not Yet

There will be nothing but night
tambourine tunes in the neighbourhood
foot-stamping emptiness-night
that is no bird which startles up
the newborn glance of Dominique
bubbles in the aquarium
quite a tenderness exists
in the dirty reed-made baskets
of hunger and thirst
perhaps the zither of native angels sounds
from the distant isles of weary eyes
hope we call it winter
not yet not yet
there is no danger
Dionysis answers the king of death
the blood of snow embraces
cloud-palmhuts
we also should investigate
the realm of comfort-stations
the fountain of the earth is leaping and giggling
remoteness is our friend
the face of decay
rolled in scent of wild thyme
nobody can hear us
we polish all alone
the rusty knives of lightning
for final reckoning

Translated by Joseph Grösz

Black Magic

There is no outlet from this sultry summer,
there is no golden gate to let me go.
When coyotes are outside, inside the lambskin
bleats as it mourns the grass which does not grow.

The magic of the spell cannot assist me,
neither the word which told me everything.
In vain I throw it, like a single die, upward;
I do not hear the magic summons ring.

You, bygone of my occupation, go on and rise as Lazarus
        did once.

I do believe I still could catch your pretty
butterfly-wings awaking from my trance.

Translated by the author

Antigenesis

the yellow rose asked of her
how old are you?
There was no answer
and yet the mountains were dressed
in nightfall's yellow
With her flower hand
she raised a cup of coffee to her lips
then all the world grew dark
as if the Creator
just finished recanting His word
before the sunflowers
even could savour the
blessings of daylight

Translated by Joseph Grosz

GEORGE VÁRHEY

At Burns Lake

For the majority of the Canadian population who live in that narrow strip that parallels the U.S. border from Montreal to Vancouver, the meaning of "wilderness" is somewhat individual. For a Montrealer it may mean the St. Henri district, or a hidden angler's cove in the Laurentians, for a Torontonian maybe a certain stretch of Jarvis St. A Vancouverite may consider Pender St. Ea., or Whistler. All the above are small letter "wilds," by far not the capital letters Wilderness, that forms the hinterland of Canada. By the same token "north" is just a direction, whereas The Canadian North is a concept. The "Footsteps" will be about this, plus a few historical facts that are not universally known.

The fact that this WILDERNESS was not explored by a Hungarian was a fluke. Spunky, younger brother of the famous Hungarian Tibet explorer, Alexander Kõrösi Csoma, was always jealous of his sibling. He searched for a long time to find an opportunity to outdo Alexander, when finally someone brought up China, as a possibility. Spunky enthusiastically accepted the challenge and either in 1786, or in 1814, but definitely in one of those centuries put together an expedition, that was financed by the Hungarian National Geographical Society. Some large firms contributed, too, among them the MFTR, that donated two ships (Tinta & Hinta) and the DDSG, that let them have an old cattle carrier, the Santa Gertrudis.

Spunky went to see an international travel agency, but the clerk spoke only French and "China" meant nothing to him. Spunky looked up the word in his dictionary, then pronounced the word "la Chine" twice, to be sure. The

Frenchman said "Aha!" (in French), then – after some run-ning to and fro – presented Spunky with several sets of maps, charts, travel documents, a Bread & Breakfast List, so the expedition took off. Everything went swimmingly, until they arrived in Lachine, Que. Spunky was devastated, but re-gained his spunk in no time. "We're here," he told his staff, "nothing we can do about it now. So let's explore Canada. Marco Polo already did China, anyway."

The equipment was unloaded, they disembarked 24 freight-mules and the exploring got underway. Alas, catas-trophe followed accidents, the mules started disappearing into large holes that appeared unexpectedly and from all sides so rapidly that it was impossible to avoid them. Spunky categorized them as "pseudovolcanic crates," the Algonquin called them "poto-ohó-oles," the Mohawks "phottô ôles" and the French missionaries of Lachine "potty holes" (in those days the entire population of Lachine and the neigh-bouring Ville Marie consisted of missionaries, who came from France's scenic Tabarnac region).

When the last mule sank in a pothole (the correct neo-English word) Spunky aborted the mission. "Let's explore something easier," he said. "New Guinea, here we come!" he added and set sail.

In the history of Quebec the potholes played an impor-tant role, they formed a quasi "Maginot Line" that foiled at least four invasion attempts by the English and Americans. Nero Wolfe English General was the only one who suc-ceeded in penetrating this formidable obstacle. His spies reported that a gigantic pothole protects Quebec City, whereupon he sent forth his engineers, who filled up the hole under cover of darkness and put a large "Plains of Abraham" signpost on it. Wolfe then formed a SWAT team from among his soldiers of Jewish origin, explained that now they have a chance to reclaim their land from the usurping Arabs and took the City-fortress with ease.

After these preliminaries I undertook the task of exploring the CANADIAN NORTH, as the second Hungarian, whose name does not yet appear in local history books.

It was 1948, when I arrived in "spot X," that is one of the least scenic outposts of the North Ontario bush. Canada paid my transportation from Innsbruck, in exchange I donated all the gold that I was going to mine in a year, to the Treasury. What a deal! No commission, no residuals, no film rights, no 85 cents an hour in wages. That was the last time I signed without an agent!

The year featured arctic cold most of the time, while the mosquitos and black flies temporarily retired into inactive status. The 40 below did not bother us deep underground, where it was balmy enough to grow flowers. During the twelve months I must have produced several tons of gold, but – when at the end of my contract I said adieu, they didn't even thank me for my loyal services.

As a free agent I tried to establish myself first in Hamilton, then in Toronto. In both places I became known as "the well to do immigrant", because I damn well had to do just about anything and everything to survive. I also hated to haggle about how often I could use the corporate jet, so, when I felt that my cup runneth over, I heeded Mr. Greeley's advice and went West.

In those days B.C. wasn't overflowing with the transferred capital of nervous Hong Kong millionaires, so there was a real shortage of work. Finally, the Employment Office came through, gave me a voucher and an airline ticket to Burns Lake (B.L.) where I was going to be Room Clerk in a hotel. "Where's Burns Lake?" I asked, whereupon the official very succintly stated: "Up North." No kidding! The plane ride to Prince George was about a thousand km., but it took another, very long bus ride to get to my destination.

After arrival I looked up my spot on the map, it turned out that I was a hop from Alaska, a skip from Yukon and a jump from NWT, alongside the road to Prince Rupert. In reality I was unimaginably far from civilization. History books list other explorers who went further north than this, but they all fell off the edge of the Earth. Before anybody cries foul I may add that all those incidents happened well before the "Round Earth Theory" was universally accepted.

An inventory of B.L. features a small lumber mill, a Royal Bank branch, my hotel, THE TWEEDSMUIR (it has been accidentally omitted from the Michelin Guide), an RCMP Post and several stores. The main industry was to equip those who – led by some strange compulsion – wanted to penetrate the unpenetrable wild. Such were sports fishermen, prospectors, gold diggers, trappers and hunters, who were after elk and their ilk. To accommodate them the Province offered TWEEDSMUIR PARK (named after Lord Tweedsmuir, who founded the Harris Knitting Mills) an about 2 million acre wilderness, cubed. There is a large signpost at the town's edge that proudly states that B.L. is the Gateway to Tweedsmuir Park.

Lacking a road network every settlement is alongside a lake, so bush pilots are able to maintain the circulation of travelers and transportation of goods. The B.C. Government is generous in this respect. Petition for a lake and you've got it. The wise town elders of B.L. asked for three. B.C. Airlines represented Burns Lake's thin lifeline to the "outside." It consisted of three DeHavilland "Beaver" six seaters and a Junkers from the 1914-18 war. The planes were flexible, one day they carried five fishermen, next day the seats were removed and they carried merchandise. The distances are so incredibly large that only the heavy and outsize stuff goes by rail or truck, everything else flies. Every lake is a year-round airport, the planes land on pontoons or skis.

At my hotel I was shown my room, the restaurant, where I fed, my realm, the reception desk and other work stations. The work was easy, the pay adequate. Food and lodging provided, I was able to transfer my checks to my Vancouver bank, intact. Cultural necessities were found in the lobby, the hotel sold newspapers, magazines and books, I read what I wanted, then just put them back on the rack.

A Hotel in a small town is always the center of social life. Everybody, who was anybody, came to meet, to eat, to drink, or just to hang around in the lobby. Soon I got to know most of the regulars, became friends with some of the bank employees, with the school teacher, formerly from Alaska, and we played penny-ante poker twice a week. All four pilots also became pals, they often hung around looking for passengers. Soon I acted as volunteer travel agent for the airline. Someone wants a ride in the bush? I'd call the hangars. They did not pay but compensated me with an occasional free ride on my days off, provided there was an empty seat.

One nice Sunday I went to the Tweedsmuir with three banker friends of mine, in a borrowed car. The approach was a dirt road, it led to a lake, where half of a dozen motorboats were tied up. We told the guard our destination, he gave us a boat and some instructions. We crossed the lake, found a similar mooring, we made the inlet on foot, there was lake No. 2 with the same setup as lake No. 1: The Chalet. Our destination was on the far side of lake No. 3.

This transportation method (boat-hike-boat) is the "portage," practiced by the French pioneers of yore, called "coureur du bois," only they carried the canoes on their backs. The lobby of the Chalet/Hunting Lodge was full of enlarged photos, where grinning fishermen show off catches of lake trout, weighing 25-30 lbs. The sight electrified us to such extent that we rented gear and a boat and started trolling. After a full day the catch was zero, that was doubly galling because our host claimed that before the chalet was built, no white man ever fished in that lake. Naturally, wealthy sportsmen do not portage-in, they fly in and out. Similarly every bit of the Chalet had to be flown in, too.

The idyllic life was interrupted by "Progress." Alcan needed more sources of energy. Cheap hydro power exists only in the wild, hence the Kemano-Kitimat project, that in sheer size compared with the building of the Panama Canal. In a nutshell, the direction of the two rivers was reversed by the erection of the then largest earthen dam, an immense lake-reservoir was created, from where a tunnel was dug to Kemano. They excavated a mountain there, to house the generators (whose cavity could accommodate the Westminster Cathedral). The power was then directed to the Kitimat smelters over a gigantic transmission-line, across the Kildala Pass. The tunnel's intake was at Tahtsa Lake and in order to get there, the Burns Lake-Emerald Glacier Mine road was extended by about forty miles.

This immense undertaking turned upside down the bucolic quiet of the wild, Burns Lake became the focal point of all works toward Tahtsa. There were only about a thousand workers at that camp, but material and equipment kept pouring in. Burns Lake, from a sleepy little hole in the wall became a bustling frontier boom-town. The hotel was filled up, the saloon was bursting at the seams with transient construction workers and transport people. The mixing of some of the elements was far from smooth. The newcomers were jeering at the bearded trappers and processors, the compliments were returned with interest and soon enough there was a wild west free-for-all.

Order was kept by the RCMP, which consisted of two

very young, boyish looking constables. We were joking that how could they arrest anyone as entry to the saloon was prohibited under 18 years.

I enjoyed watching the melees from a safe distance. One time the saloon bouncer kicked out six drunken prospectors, who then continued imbibing on an empty lot nearby. Soon one of them keeled over, whereupon the others tried to revive him. He did not budge, so one of them diagnosed the poor creature dead. The others took terms in attempting different reviving procedures without any result. He was then declared officially dead and the subject of the next palaver was the appropriate funeral. One of them proposed internment, but they had no spades to dig a grave. That really threw them for a loop, what kind of gold diggers were they? They consulted their flasks and, sure enough, the inspiration came. One of them suggested cremation. After some discussion they started to gather dead branches. When the pyre was high enough they attempted to place the "cadaver" on top of it. Here I thought the farce went too far. I asked the porter to call the gendarmes, who duly came and placed the mourners in the cooler until they sobered up.

The monotony of daily grind is interrupted by the appearance of a young lady in a skirt and heels. She traipses to my desk, declares that she is a reporter of the Prince Rupert Bugle, declares that her editor heard about the tremendous boom in B.L. and she's to write an article about it. And she needs accommodation. (I almost gave her the honeymoon suite.) Told her that there was no vacancy as every room's been reserved three months in advance. When she started to beg me I gave her directions to a tent and sleeping-bag store. She was so depressed that I took pity on her and gave her a room. I invited Mabel (can't remember her real name) to lunch and confessed that I wasn't really a hotelman, but a correspondent of Reuters and I'd been sent here with the same appointment as she. I made brief references to my previous work in London, Paris and Cairo, at the latter being a camel driver and in Venice where I poled a gondola. Mabel was impressed.

I really went all out for the reporter. I introduced her to all the important people worthy of an interview. In a few days she filled her book with facts, material, background, perspective, interviews. I should have encouraged her to leave it at that. Hell, no. I started to feed her with all the frivolous "events": the wild-west free-for-all in the saloon. The baby-faced mounties who are too young to enter the bar for arrest; the drunken prospector on the funeral pyre. It was a fatal error, but I had to outdo myself. I added that the peace-loving populace is fed up with the frontier-town atmosphere and "progress" and there is a movement afoot whereby the "Gateway to Tweedsmuir Park" sign will be repainted to read GET AWAY FROM T.P.

Mabel returned home and everything went back to normal, the days became routine again. But for two weeks only. One morning Mr. C., the hotel manager, asks me to come to his office. "There is," he tells me, "Mr. B., the owner of the hotel and the saw mill."

Mr. B. is red as a beet, he is pounding on Mr. C.'s desk with a newspaper, screaming at me: "Would you please look at this article and comment on it!"

I look, and find that it is the Prince Rupert paper. There is a full-page story under Mabel's byline. The large print headline says: THE WILD WEST IS ALIVE AND WELL IN BURNS LAKE.

I am utterly devastated. Mabel gave two short paragraphs to the real story, the rest is based on my last-day-addition, even more blown up! Then there are the cartoons! One shows a mountie in diapers, pacifier in his mouth beckoning to a bearded gorilla in the bar: "Come on out, I want to arrest you!" Another cartoon shows the mourning prospectors around the funeral pyre.

In the article I am described as a ". . . European observer, the Hotel's highly respected room clerk, who's beside himself of sheer joy that his favourite childhood books about the Wild West became a reality in B.L. . . ." At the end of the article there is another cartoon, showing the GATEWAY sign crossed out and GET AWAY substituted.

According to Mr. B. I libeled the town, ruined the hotel's reputation, besmirched the RCMP and dishonoured him personally. He ended the tirade by inviting me to be first, who gets away from Burns Lake. I'm unceremoniously fired.

The story got out, most people – with a bit of sense of humour – laughed their head off. Among them was Mr. Scott, manager of the Emerald Glacier Mine, who happened to be at the hotel that day. He tells me, that his Administrative Officer has just resigned. "Would you consider to take his place?" When he said that the pay would be almost the double of that what I earned in the hotel, I accepted without any hesitation.

And Mabel? I had hoped her next assignment was to write a humorous article about Beirut.

GYÖRGY VITÉZ

At the Station

The first of the lemmings has a cap on his head.
He sits on his stylish valise, clutching a golfbag.
"Is it true, is it true," he inquires mechanically,
"that the sea is deep, cold, wide, and salty?"

Affirmative replies follow like beads on a rosary.
He listens attentively. "Terrible times are upon us,"
he exclaims, rising and racing along the platform.
Predictably, the crowd follows him.
Those in the third and fourth rows are without valises.
Even the bare-headed join the race of the rodents.
No clubs or ironbars are driving them.

"Undisciplined scum," exclaims the station-master.
"They will be too late for the express to Kiruna."
Of course they are late. Of course they continue, on foot,
until they reach the sea which they find to be
(of course) deep, cold, wide, salty – and furious.

English version by John Robert Colombo

Love

As for flesh: a patchwork quilt
of blue bites brown bruises red welts pink eruptions

as for flesh: a powdery smoothness of pale topography (in
   relief)

well mapped but not yet exposed; a chain of colonial
    countries
darkly dismembered in harshest light (the crocodiles,
    vaulting Sun)

as for flesh: there is the dryness of noon
evening's sweat the viscid night rain (and sharp smell of
    sunrise)

as for flesh: finger and tongue swallowing
tightening: traps and a hint of extracurricular hurt
as for flesh: the withdrawal is temporary.

as for the soul: a question mark parachuting down to earth
a sweet potato peeled from her evening gown

as for the soul: the sword flashes forth bright faces
and the cunning blade sprouts where its hilt ought to be.

English version by John Robert Colombo

Churchmusic

"Look to thy resting place," Johann Sebastian Bach
    proposed,
Bestelle dein Haus – an acceptable offer, put this way:
Gentleman – musicians in tails keep kissing their flutes:
Fellatio ad absurdum.
From the balcony it seems the cellist's hair brushes the
    floor
– Johanna Sebastiana Rapunzel
raise us up clutching your grey shaggy wig
(but where have we got to, with our historical recreations

– our place in history? – conducting from the harpsichord
that rings our hangovers?)
an elegant, curlicued Baroque passing:
we dream you dream they dream,
the choristers primly peck about and knock their
sparrow heads together in the dusty barnyard of their
    scores,
tip-top-toeing notebirds
out of their cages into the heavens urgently urging!
Even the first violin
spreads his swallow tail
takes wing
and flies away.

Translated by George Payerle

Mercier Bridge

An unpolished orange moon, towed by great cables
through the smooth black sky between two radio towers,
swings, swollen and disgusting. From aerial steel
red eyes blink, stare. Sliding upward, she stifles stars,
becomes more small, more perfect, as she pulls away from
    earth.
The car turns onto the bridge. The river beneath
bounces blue, green, lilac balls. The distilleries' breath
clouds the surface reflections. The headlights of cars,
a double string of pearls, twines and pulls on the bare
black throat of this once royal city. The dwindling traveller
pales. Stiff shadows shift on the back seats. And the world,
inanimate, grows more perfect than its makers.

English version by Robin Skelton

ROBERT ZEND

Oab's Lullaby

Sleep Zend, sleep
your dreamless sleep,
sleep in my strong arms,
you will look at me no more
you will smother me no more

you will plan me no more,
play with me no more
your sleep will be soft,

I would like to tell you

I would like to show you

that you did not know me
that you misconceived me,

You thought you made me,
with your loving word-care,
you called me your little One,
you called me your Creature,
and you were always wrong,

You thought you could
          leave me
saying farewell to me
undertaking new journeys,
you never reckoned
a black gate awaits you,
a waveless ocean,

sleep, Zend, sleep
your morningless sleep,
in my white silence,
with your worried eyes
with your warming
          heartbeats,
remember me no more,
and love me no more,
your sleep will be deep –

– though you hear me
          no more –
– though you see me
          no more –
from the beginning,
misunderstood me.

you thought you formed me,
your caressing pen-strokes,
your Offspring, your Art,
your Symbol, your Love,
my poor, dear Zend . . .

once you had finished me,

then going on your way,
toward new adventures . . .
that at the end of your road
a bottomless throat,
a castle with no exit . . .

you planned me as a short
        affair
you saw your road stretching
now stiff and with closed eyes
and the endless road is
        stretching
You misunderstood me
you thought you had
        created me
you felt you invented me

you believed that you'd
        written me
It was I who wanted
        to be born
and I became you
Through aeons I came
        to you
from the four or more
light-year-sized galaxies
when, finally, I first whispered
Now, shrunk and pale,
on my soft pages,
never having grasped
never having conjectured
never knowing the secret

Ardô did not create you
you created him
Likewise I must be wrong
stretching endlessly
        ahead of me
it's Irdu who created me,
it's Irdu who will carry me

one among your many books,

endlessly ahead of you –
you lie on my pages
ahead of me, not you.

never even knowing it
thought it was I who
        found you,
though it was I who attacked
        your mind,
though it was I who
used your hand as my tool.
because it was I who had
        to be
not you I (as you thought).
wading through endless
        times,
corners of the world,
whirled and thundered
my name into your ear –
you lie in my arms,
in my white silence,
in inconceivable truth,
the incredible reality,
that I now reveal to you:

although he thought he did:
as I created you.
when I see my road
as once you saw yours:

I was just his tool,
for he created me!

And this is how we
        all have been
for, see, Zend, we all go
remembering the future
Pictures to painters,
melodies to composers
as unborn souls spotting
select their parents
so float the works of Man
spotting stormy vortexes
to be brought to life
It is the finished creature
towards its fragment-creator

wrong, all the time,

from the future to the past,
and planning the past.
statues to sculptors,
and poems to poets,
tempests of lust
by whom they'll be conceived,
searching for creators,
of inspiration
by the author they choose.
that marches from the future
who roves in the past.

This is the secret,
the eye of the mind
it sees the past as rock
but beyond the veil
real time

the great mystery:
reverses time,
sees the future as mist,
which curtains the mind,
flows backward –

Thus came I too
into the fog of the past
and now I'm carrying you
to the domain where there are
where there are no words
        found
no struggles, no doubts,
to the land of winter

from the petrified future
where I found you, Zend,
back to where I came from,
no uncertainties,
no decisions to be
        made,
no threats and no hopes,
from where once I came
        to you,

to the land of gods,
fleshless and bloodless

motionless, eternal,
and noiseless gods –

Sleep, Zend, sleep,
frozen and changeless,
not knowing the secret,

restless soul, rest now,
numb and deaf, sleep,
lifeless as the gods,

sleep in my strong arms,
I take you to my land
because in my land
you'll be just a name,
a structure, a pattern,
filled with my spirit
on the shelves of libraries,
without worrying
without craving
and you'll be remembered
as you were remembered
remembered or forgotten,
remembered or forgotten,
remembered or forgotten,
for in the mouth of eternity these two words are one –

in my white silence . . .
where you'll never die
you'll never be alive,
a title, an idea,
a unique combination,
you shall be me
in the depth of future minds,
for posterity,
for immortality,
by eternity
even before birth,

BIOGRAPHICAL NOTES

This section contains brief biographical summaries of authors represented in this anthology. For a comprehensive coverage please see: J. Miska: *Literature of Hungarian-Canadians*. Toronto: Rákóczi Foundation, 1994.

Béky-Halász, Iván: He was born in Budapest in 1919 and received his university education in that city. Came to Canada in 1956, obtained a degree in Library Science at the University of Toronto and worked in the John P. Robarts Research Library. He has published seven collections of poems, including *Arccal a falnak* (Facing the Wall, 1972), *Áldott kiköktök* (Blessed Harbours, 1979), *Indián nyár* (Indian Summer, 1981), and translated into English the work of several Hungarian poets. He returned to Budapest permanently, where he passed away in 1997.

Bisztray, George: Born in 1938 in Budapest, received his M.A. at the University of Budapest in 1962 and a Ph.D. in comparative literature at the University of Minnesota. Before his appointment to the Chair of Hungarian Studies at the University of Toronto, he has taught at the universities of Minnesota, Chicago, and Alberta. Founder of the Hungarian Studies Association of Canada and author and editor of several books and monographs, including *Marxist Model of Literary Realism* (1978), and *Hungarian Canadian Literature* (1981).

Csinger, Joseph: Born in Hungary in 1923, he left the country for France in 1948 and came to Canada in 1951. He has published poetry in Hungarian and English periodicals. Published three collections of poems, *Emlékvitorla* (Memory Sailboat, 1997), *Keyhole in the Sky* (1998), and *Urrepülés* (Space Travel, 2000).

Dancs, Rose: Author, editor, publisher, born in Transylvania, Romania. She came to Canada in 1988 and continued her education at the University of Toronto. Her stories, essays and review articles on literature, history and art have appeared in periodicals and newspapers. Published a collection of stories and essays, *Vaddisznók törték a törökbúzát* (Wild boars Were Plundering the Corn, 2000). Editor of *Kaleidoscope*, a monthly periodical in Hungarian and English. She lives in Toronto.

Dobozy, Tamas: Second-generation writer, he has completed his Ph.D. degree in literature at the University of British Columbia. His work has appeared in journals. His novel *Doggone* was published by Gutter Press in 1998 and his short story, "Like a Salmon Getting Me Down," won the sub-TERRAIN 1995 short fiction contest. He has lived in Vancouver, Montreal, Budapest and Toronto

Domokos, Alex: Born in 1921 in Szabadka (now Yugoslavia). Spent several years in prisoner of war camps in the Soviet Union and forced labour camps in Hungary. Came to Canada in 1956 and has lived in Winnipeg ever since, where he authored several novels and books of short stories, poems and plays, including *A római százados* (The Roman Soldier, 1994), *Új Prometheus* (New Prometheus, 1998). Some of his writings have also appeared in English translation and are available on Internet. A recepient of several awards for literature and amateur film productions. He lives in Winnipeg.

Dósa, Csaba: A member of the younger generation, Dósa was born in Transylvania. He published poetry and short fiction in *Krónika*, *Arkánum* and other periodicals. One of his most significant short prose is "Védtelenség" (Defencelessness) demonstrates an outstanding gift for metaphor. He lives in Toronto.

Faludy, George: Eminent author and scholar, born in 1910 in Budapest. He has lived in France, Morocco, the United States, England, and Canada. He has published twenty collections of poetry, memoirs, translations and scholarly works. Recepient of an honorary doctorate degree from the University of Toronto and was twice nominated for the Nobel Prize in literature. He has relocated to Hungary and lives in Budapest.

Farkas, Endre: Born in 1948 in Hajdúnánás, Hungary. Came to Canada in 1956. Published several books of poetry (*Szervusz*, 1976, *Romantic at Heart and Other Faults*, 1979, *How to . . .* , 1988), and edited three anthologies. Published poems in periodicals, and gives readings and video performances. His motto is: "I write to remember.

I write to map the sacred geography. I write to do something useless in the world obsessed with utility. And through the act, I exercise the most fundamental human right: the right of the private voice to speak out . . ."

Fáy, Ferenc: Born in 1921 in Pécel, Hungary and served as an officer in the Royal Hungarian Army. Left his native land in 1948 and came to Toronto, where he lived until his death in 1980. He has published seven collections of poetry, including *Jeremiás siralmai* (The Lamentations of Jeremiah, 1956), *Az írást egyszer megtalálják* (They Are Going to Find the Writing One Day, 1959), *Magamsirató* (Self-lamentation, 1967), *Összegyujtött versek* (Collected Poems, 1982).

Gottlieb, Paul: A hungarian-born Canadian writer, his first novel *Agency,* became a national best-seller and was made into a movie. He also wrote the screenplay of In Praise of Older Owmen, based on Stephen Vizinczey's world-wide best seller. Paul has worked mostly in advertising and films, as well as teaching at Sheridan and Seneca Colleges. He has been a visiting professor at Eotvos Lorand University, The Economics University of Budapest, as well as at Jozsef Attila university, Szeged. His most recent work is the original English translation of Szabo Istvan's script "Sunshine," winner of the 1999 Genie Award for Best Picture.

Green, Maria: Born in 1922 in Arad (now Romania) and received her education in Budapest. Came to Canada in 1956. Attended the University of British Columbia and the University of Washington (Ph.D.). Taught French literature at the University of Saskatchewan, Saskatoon. Authored, edited or translated several research papers and monographs. She also translates short stories by fellow Hungarian authors into English.

Hajós, Tamás: Born in 1953 in Budapest. In Canada he has published poems in anthologies and put out a collection of poems: *Szárítókötélen* (On the Clothesline, 1982). His writings in English translation have appeared in *WRIT/FOR 1982 Translations.*

Jonas, George: Born in 1935 in Budapest. He came to Canada in 1956 and settled in Toronto. His has published books of poems (*The Absolute Smile*, 1967, *The Happy Hungry Man*, 1970, *Cities*, 1973,

East Wind Blows West, 1993), his essays and articles have appeared in periodicals, his television and radio plays have been broadcast by CBC TV and Radio. He has also published and co-authored novels, biographies, legal books, librettos and other material. He lives in Toronto.

Kalman, Judith: Born in Budapest and came to Canada via London, after 1956. Her writing has appeared in periodicals and anthologies. Recipient of a number of literary awards. Her book of linked stories, *The County of Birches*, published by Douglas & McIntire in 1998, was also published in the United States. She lives in Toronto.

Kemenes Géfin, László: Born in Szombathely, Hungary. Came to Montreal in 1957. Received a Ph.D. degree from Concordia University, taught English literature at the same institute. His poems have appeared in periodicals and anthologies. He is co-editor of the periodical *Arkánum*, and editor of *A nyugati magyar költők antológiája*. He has published five collections of poetry, including *Jégvirág* (Ice Flower, 1966), *Zenit* (Zenith, 1969), *Pogány diaszpóra* (Pagan Diaspora, 1975), and the *Fehérlófia* (Son of a White Horse) collections. He translated into Hungarian Ezra Pound's *Cantos*. He lives in The Netherlands.

Konyves, Tom: An avant-garde poet, and former editor of *Hh* (*Hobyhorse*), director of *Poetry Véhicule*, and secretary for *Véhicule Art* (Montreal). Spent several years with Québecois artists in Montreal, documenting their work on videotape for a series entitled Art Montréal. Contributed poems to periodicals and published several collections, including *No Parking* (1978), *Poetry in Performance* (1982), and *Ex Perimeter.*(1988).

Marlyn, John: Distinguished novelist and playwright, born in 1912 in Nagybecskerek (now Yugoslavia). Came to Canada as a child with his parents and settled in Winnipeg, the source of his novels, *Under the Ribs of Death* (1957, 1961), and *Putzi, I Love You, You Little Square* (1982). He has lived in the United Kingdom, taught drama at Carleton University, and published short stories and plays in periodicals. Received the Beta Sigma Phi First Novel Award in 1958, a Canada Foundation Award in 1958, two Canada Council Senior Arts Awards in 1969 and 1976, and an Ontario Arts Council Award in 1975. The short story reproduced in this collection is an excerpt from his new novel to be published shortly.

McDougall Mezey, Marina: Born in 1945 in Budapest, left Hungary for Canada in 1956. Attended McGill University. She served as program coordinator for the Organization for Economic Cooperation and Development in Paris, followed by appointments as translator and interpreter for various companies in Zurich and Toronto. Edited *Current Magazine* and contributed papers and juvenile fiction to various periodicals and newspapers in Canada. Received the Vicky Metcalf Short Story Award. Published *Little Rooster's Diamond Penny* (1978).

Payerle, George: Born of Hungarian parents in Vancouver in 1945 and received a B.A. and an M.A. degree from UBC. He spoke only Hungarian until he entered the school system, and thus considers himself a "native D.P." Published poems, short stories and translations from Hungarian into English, as well as novels (*The Afterpeople*, 1970, *Wolfbane Fane*, 1977, the latest, from which the "London Scenes" was taken, *Unknown Soldier*.)

Porter, Anna: Prominent novelist, publisher, and Officer of the Order of Canada, born Anna Maria Szigethy in Budapest. Participated in the Hungarian uprising of 1956. Escaped the country in 1957, finding refuge in Christchurch, N.Z., where she studied English literature at the University of Canterbury (B.A., M.A.). After a two-year stint in England, she moved to Toronto and worked for Collier Macmillan Canada and McClelland & Stewart, at the latter as Vice President and Editor-in-Chief (until 1979). Since 1982 she is CEO and director of Key Porter Books. She has published four novels: *Hidden Agenda* (1985); *Mortal Sins* (1987); *The Bookfair Murders* (1997), and *The Storyteller* (2000).

Sajgó, Szabolcs: Born in 1951 in Budapest, where he was ordained a priest of the Roman Catholic Church. He came to Canada in 1982. His poems have appeared in *Vigilia, Krónika, Nyugati Magyarság* and *Nyugtalan Tengerszem*, an anthology. Published a collection of poems, *Elárvult látomás* (Betrayed Apparition, 1987). He is co-editor of the periodical *Szív*. He has returned to Hungary and lives in Budapest.

Sandor, Karl: Born in 1931 in Budapest and came to Canada in 1957.

His literary career was inspired by Beckett, Durrenmatt and Boris Vian. His poems, short stories and plays have appeared in magazines and anthologies and were broadcast on CBC Radio. He lives in Vancouver.

Sárvári, Éva: Born in 1931 in Budapest. Left Hungary in 1956 and came to Canada a decade later via Denmark and Australia. She has published short stories in magazines, and four novels, *Kigyúlt a fény* (The Light Goes On, 1972), *Félúton* (Halfway, 1975), *Messze délen* (Faraway in the South, 1976), and *Egy tál arany a szivárvány végén* (A Platter of Gold at the Foot of the Rainbow,1994). She lives in Toronto.

Seres, József: Born in 1942 in Szerencs, Hungary, received his education in Miskolc and Szeged. He continued his studies in sculpting at the Ontario College of Arts in Toronto and graduated in 1979. His poems have appeared in magazines and anthologies, and some of them were set to music and performed on stage in Hungary and Canada. Published two books of poems, *Évszakok nélkül* (Without Seasons, 1978) *Légy vendégem* (Be My Guest, 2000).

Simándi, Ágnes: Born in 1954 in Budapest and attended the Péter Pázmány Theological Academy. She came to Toronto in 1987 and continued her education at the University of Toronto, Trinity College (M.Div., 1991). Her poems have appeared in periodicals in Budapest, Chicago, Toronto, and Vancouver. Published three books of poetry: *Nárciszok évada* (A Season of Narcisses, 1987), *Tiltott játék* (Forbidden Play, 1993), and . . . *csak kisérlet, közelítés*, (. . . experiment and Approach, 1998). She lives in Toronto.

Szohner, Gabriel: Born in 1936 in Budapest, he came to Canada in 1956. His first short stories and poems began to appear in Hungarian-Canadian newspapers. Received a Canada Council grant to complete *The Immigrant*, published in 1977. His short stories and poems written in English have appeared in Western News, Canadian Fiction Magazine and other periodicals. He lives in Vancouver.

Tallosi, Jim: Born in Dunakeszi, Hungary, in 1947, and came to Canada in 1956. A graduate of the University of Winnipeg and the author of two books of poetry, *The Trapper and the Fur-faced Spirits* (1981) and *Talking Water, Talking Fire* (1985). His poems have appeared in *Mandala, Poetry of Manitoba, Prairie Fire and NewWest*

Review. In his more recent poems he has refined his craft to create timeless and exquisite epiphanies.

Tamási, Miklós: Born in Hungary and received his formal education in that country. He came to Canada in 1956 and settled in Vancouver. He was an active member of the Hungarian community until his death in 1994. Founding editor of the monthly periodical *Tárogató*, he contributed articles, plays and poems to various newspapers and journals. His poems were published in three collections, including *Eszkimó szerelem* (Eskimo Love, 1977) and *Totemfák* (Totem-poles, 1994).

Tihanyi, Eva: Born in Budapest in 1956 and came to Canada with her parents at the age of six. Attended the University of Windsor, she taught English for seven years at the Humber, George Brown, and Seneca Colleges in Toronto, and the University of Windsor. She lives in Welland, Ont., where she is a Professor English at Niagara College. She has published four books of poetry, *A Sequence of Blood* (1982), *Prophesies Near the Speed of Light* (1984), *Saved by the Telling* (1995), and *Restoring the Wickedness* (2000).

Toth, Nancy: Born in 1947 in Prince Albert, Sask. She has an M.A. and A.B.D. (All but dissertation) for the Ph.D. in English from the University of Alberta. She lives in Edmonton where she works as a Human Resources Manager. She has published poems and reviews in several Canadian periodicals. Her poems inspired dance, music and song in other Alberta artists and were read on stage, radio and television. A collection of her poems *Pattern Without End*, was published in 1979. Some of her poems were translated into Hungarian by Robert Zend and published in *Mozgó* Világ (Budapest).

Tuz, Tamás: Real name: Lajos Makkó, born in 1916 in Győr, where he was ordained a priest of the Roman Catholic Church. During the Second World War he served as a military chaplain in the Hungarian Army and spent three years in prisoner of war camps in the U.S.S.R. Came to Canada in 1956. Published more than twenty volumes of poetry, including *Nyugtalan szárnyakon* (On Restless Wings, 1959), *Angyal, mondd ki csak félig* (Angel, Reveal Only Half of It, 1975), *Hét sóhaj a hegyen* (Seven Sighs on the Mountain, 1987). Also published novels and a book of stories. He died in 1992.

Várhey, George: Born in 1921 in Budapest and attended the Elizabeth University of Pécs, majoring in law. During the war he served in the Royal Hungarian Army. Came to Canada in 1948 and was employed by various commercial firms. His articles and stories have appeared in periodicals and newspapers. His novel: *The Baroque Triangle* is in manuscript. "At Burns Lake" is an excerpt from a three-volume biographical novel still in manuscript. He lives in Montreal.

Vitéz, György: Real name: György Németh. Chief psychologist at the Queen Elizabeth Hospital in Montreal and adjunct assistant professor of psychology at Concordia University. Born in 1933 in Budapest and came to Canada in 1956. He attended Sir George Williams University and McGill University (M.A. and Ph.D.). Co-editor of *Arkánum* an avant-garde periodical and contributor to several journals. Translated into Hungarian the poetry of William Carlos Williams. Published four collections of poetry: *Amerikai történet* (An American Story, 1977), *Missa agnostica* (1979), *jel beszéd* (Sign Language, 1982), *Az ájtatos manó imája* (The Prayer of the Mantis, 1991), *Haza Tér És* (Home-ComIng, 1998), and *Confabulatio mystica* (2001), the last three collections were published in Hungary.

Zend, Robert: Born in 1929 in Budapest, graduated from the Péter Pázmány University. Came to Toronto in 1956, where he has lived until his death in 1985. Worked for the Canadian Broadcasting Corporation. His poems appeared in periodicals and anthologies. Published several books of poems in English and Hungarian, including *From Zero to One* (1973), *Beyond Labels* (1982), *Oab* (1985), *Three Roberts* (1985), *Fából vaskarikatúrák* (1993).

SOURCES OF LITERATURE

This compilation includes a select list of publications in the English language. For a comprehensive coverage of the subject the user should consult *Canadian Studies on Hungarians*, a bibliographic series of four volumes (1987-1998), by John Miska.

REFERENCE SOURCES

Bisztray, George. *Hungarian-Canadian Literature*. Toronto: University of Toronto Press, 1985. 116 p.

[A comprehensive study of the history and the various schools of Hungarian-Canadian poetry, fiction, drama and essay literature. Includes an extensive bibliography on the subject, pp. 85-116. A basic reference tool.]

Miska, John. *Canadian Studies on Hungarians 1886-1986: An Annotated Bibliography of Primary and Secondary Sources*. Regina: Canadian Plains Research Center, University of Regina, 1987. 245 pp. Supplements: Ottawa, 1992; Budapest 1995, Toronto and Budapest, 1998.

[A comprehensive compilation of more than 2000 references to Hungarian studies.]

Miska, John. *Ethnic and Native Canadian Literature. A Bibliography*. Toronto: University of Toronto Press, 1990. 445 p.

[Provides references to 600 publications pertaining to Hungarian-Canadian literature.]

Miska, John. *Literature of Hungarian Canadians*. Toronto: Rákóczi Foundation, 1991. 143 p.

[A collection of four essays and a bibliography of more than 600 references to books of literary works, research studies, university dissertations and review articles. Biographical notes on 90 authors are provided.]

Széplaki, Joseph. *Hungarians in the United States and Canada: A*

Bibliography. Minneapolis: University of Minnesota, Immigration History Research Center, 1977. 113 p.

[Includes the works of several Hungarian-Canadian writers.]

Young, Judy. "Some Thoughts about the Present State of Bibliography in the Area of Canadian Ethnic Studies." Pages 38-47 in: *Bibliography for Canadian Studies: Present Trends and Future Needs/ Bibliographie pour les Études Canadiennes: situation actuelle et besoins futurs. Proceedings of a Conference Held at Dalhousie University, Halifax, N.S., June 1-2, 1991.* Ed. A.B. Piternick. Willowdale, Ont.: Association for Canadian Studies, 1981.

[A summary of bibliographic trends in Canadian literature in languages other than English and French. Several sources of Hungarian interest are cited and analyzed.]

RESEARCH STUDIES

Bisztray, George. "Canadian-Hungarian Literature: Values Lost and Found." Pages 22-35 in: *Identifications: Ethnicity and the Writer in Canada.* Ed. Jars Balan. Edmonton: The Canadian Institute of Ukrainian Studies, The University of Alberta, 1982.

Kadar, Marlene. "Reading Ethnicity into Life Writing: Out from 'Under the Ribs of Death' and into the 'Light Chaos' – Béla Szabados's Narrator Rewrites Sándor Hunyadi." *Essays on Canadian Writing 57* (Winter 1995): 70-83.

[An analytical essay relating to ethnic Canadian writing, offering as a case study the novels of John Marlyn and Béla Szabados.]

Kirkconnell, Watson. "A Canadian Meets the Magyars." *Canadian-American Review of Hungarian Studies I*, nos. 1-2 (1974): 1-14.

[Reference is made to several Hungarian-Canadian authors, including Sándor Domokos, Ferenc Fáy, László Kemenes Géfin, János Miska and György Vitéz.]

Kovács, M.L. "Early Hungarian Canadian Culture." *Canadian-American Review of Hungarian Studies VII*, no. 1 (1980): 55-76.

[A study of early Hungarian-Canadian literary trends in Saskatchewan during the first part of the 1900s. Includes excerpts from the work of pioneer Hungarian poets and fiction writers translated into English by the author.]

Miska, John. "Modern Hungarian Poetry in Canada." *Canadian-American Review of Hungarian Studies VII*, no. 1 (1980): 77-83.
[Introduces the poetry of Ferenc Fáy, Tamás Tuz, László Kemenes Géfin, György Vitéz and many others.]

Naves Kalman, Elaine. "New World Hybrids." *Montreal Gazette* (May 18, 1996): 11.
[The revolution of 1956 affects Hungarian writers György Vitéz and László Kemenes Géfin who fled and established themselves as poets in Montreal.]

Palmer, Tamara. "Ethnic Response to the Canadian Prairies (1900-1950): A Literary Perspective on Perceptions of the Physical and Social Environment." *Prairie Forum* 12 no 1 (1978): 49-73.
[Areas studied: prairie novels and the environment's influence on the authors, including John Marlyn.]

Papp de Carrington, Ildiko. "From 'Hunky' to Don Juan: The Changing Hungarian Identity in Canadian Fiction." *Canadian Literature 89* (1981): 33-44.
[A study of Hungarian prose writing encompassing the novels of John Marlyn, Marika Robert, Stephen Vizinczey, and short stories by János Miska, István Nagy and László Szilvássy.]

Tötösy de Zepetnek, Steven. "Literary Theory, Ethnic Minority Writing, and Systemic and Empirical Approach." *Canadian Ethnic Studies 23* no 3 (1996): 100-106.
[Describes the framework and the methodology of the Systemic and Empirical Approach to literature, with emphasis upon Canadian – Hungarian and Hungarian writing.]

Tötösy de Zepetnek, Steven. "Political Satire in Hungarian Exile Literature: Systemic Considerations." Pages 250-255 in: *The Search for a New Alphabet: Literary Studies in a Changing World, in Honor of Douwe Fokkema*. Ed. Harald Hendrix et al. Amsterdam: John Benjamins, 1996.
[A systemic study of the poetry of László Kemenes Géfin and Robert Zend.]

Young, Judy. "'Amid Alien Corn': An Unrecognized Dimension of

Canadian Literature." Pages 171-182 in: *Second Banff Conference of Central and East European Studies of Canada. Banff, Alta., March 2-5, 1978.* Edmonton: CEESAC, 1978.

[Discusses the shortcomings experienced by Canadian authors of ethnic origin. Several Hungarians are mentioned.]

Young, Judy. "Canadian Literature in the Non-Official Languages: A Review of Recent Publications and Work in Progress." *Canadian Ethnic Studies XIV*, no 1 (1982): 138-149.

[A summary of poetry and fiction, anthologies and bibliographical works. Several Hungarian publications are mentioned.]

John Miska is a librarian by profession but he is also known for his books of stories, essays, anthologies and translations published in Hungarian and English. His bibliography, *Ethnic and Native Canadian Literature*, put out by the University of Toronto Press (1990), is considered to be a pioneer work. His *Canadian Studies on Hungarians*, published by the Canadian Plains Research Center, University of Regina (1987), and its three supplements (Ottawa, 1992, Budapest, 1995, and Toronto-Budapest, 1998), are a major source of information in Canadian Hungarology. Founder of the Hungarian-Canadian Authors' Association (1968), he is one of the prime movers of Hungarian literature in Canada. He has published a series of books on the accomplishments of Hungarian scientists, scholars, educators, artists and writers in Canada that earned him several university and government grants, as well as such awards as the Queen's Jubilee Silver Medal, the Alberta Achievement Award for Excellence in Literature, and a silver and gold medal from the Árpád Academy, Cleveland, OH. Since his retirement in 1991, he has edited for five years the Vancouver-based periodical *Tárogató*.

MEMBRE DE SCABRINI MEDIA

Québec, Canada
2002